ALL PETS GO TO HEAVEN

The Spiritual Lives of the Animals We Love

SYLVIA BROWNE

Doubleday Large Print
Home Library Edition

A FIRESIDE BOOK
Published by Simon & Schuster

NEW YORK   LONDON   TORONTO   SYDNEY

Fireside
A Division of Simon & Schuster, Inc.
1230 Avenue of the Americas
New York, NY 10020

Interior illustrations by Jan Mucklestone

Manufactured in the United States of America

ISBN-13: 978-1-60751-479-4

**This Large Print Book carries the
Seal of Approval of N.A.V.H.**

To my current precious darlings—

Balooga, Biscuit, Troy, Sasha,
and Soldier—

**for being a constant reminder of God's
unconditional love and many blessings, and for helping me to start each
day with a smile.**

And to my past beloved pets—

Kristen, Misty, Chewy, Mitzy, Jolie, Thor,
Crystal, Flower, and many others

**from this and my many past lives—
with whom I look forward to being reunited when it's my time to go Home.**

ACKNOWLEDGMENTS

To all those who have loved and lost their beloved pets and a special acknowledgment and thank you to all those who thoughtfully shared their heartfelt stories with me.

CONTENTS

ALL PETS GO TO HEAVEN

1

ANIMALS IN OUR LIVES

"We will be known forever by the
tracks we leave."
—**Dakota Indian proverb**

For my entire career as a professional psychic, people have come to me asking questions about everything in their lives— their jobs, their families, their relationships, and their futures. But one question comes up time and again: *What happens to my beloved pet when he dies?* People want to be assured that their dog or cat or bird or horse—creatures they love just as much as any human in their life—will find peace in the afterlife.

I am here to tell you that all pets *do* go to heaven. I will also explain to you the extraordinary abilities that pets have here on earth that we're just beginning to understand and acknowledge. These abilities lead us to amazing stories of the bonds between humans and the animals they love, experiences with animals both in this world and on the Other Side, which reaffirm the remarkable relationships we have with our precious pets.

Since before recorded history, humankind has always had a relationship with animals, whether it was for sustenance, protection, worship, or to give service. Gradually over time many of the animals encountered by humans were domesticated and formed either a loving partnership with us as pets or were put into service to help humankind in its work or as a food source. We even see when animals are taken to visit the elderly how that person's blood pressure goes down and any depression subsides. I'm convinced animals can neutralize negative energy without ever absorbing it as we do. That's why I've even referred to them as a form of guardian angel on this planet.

The stories that follow will show the different facets of what animals do and can do and how sentient they are. Whether it's just your dear pet and protectorate or your own totem (which we will get to later), we will see how animals have saved lives and even see and feel things that we cannot see or feel such as seeing spirits or alerting us to fire or even earthquakes long before we are aware of such things. Humankind has just begun to scratch the surface of the great intelligence our animals have, and hopefully you will get a deeper insight into the sometimes complex minds of our beloved friends in the animal kingdom. This book will explore through research as well as personal stories the help, bravery, love, and loyalty these wondrous creatures afford us.

They are not dead who live in the hearts they leave behind.
—TUSCARORA

WHEN WE LOSE A PET

Most animal lovers have a pet, and those pets quickly become a part of their families. When a beloved pet passes away, a huge void is left in your family, not to mention your heart. It makes me furious when someone is grieving over the loss of a pet and they hear the words, "Well, after all it was only an animal!" When these words have been uttered to me, rather than froth at the mouth I usually try to simply walk away. As I've grown older I've tried to be more tolerant and say to myself that these people just don't know; they are simply ignorant of the love and richness that our pets lend to our lives.

We will expand on the subject of pet loss later, but right now I want to tell you about my Jolie. Jolie was a West Highland terrier and the most active, funny, and caring dog I have ever known. She was one of my dearest pets, and I had her for nine wonderful years. One day I got a call at work that Jolie had suddenly keeled over and was nonresponsive. My youngest, psychic son, Chris, ran over and gave her some resuscitation by pushing on her rib cage, and by the time I got home she was sitting up, but with a glazed look on her face. I immediately noticed she was terribly bloated, and we raced her to the vet. After a whole battery of tests he told me grimly that the news wasn't good. Jolie was suffering from severe heart failure.

He explained that the symptoms are similar to those experienced by people who have heart attacks or strokes. Jolie, he said, was filling up with water so fast she would drown in her own fluid. I had to put her to sleep. He suggested that I leave the room, but I wouldn't—I wanted my eyes to be the last thing Jolie saw.

The shot was administered, and I truly felt like she was saying, *it's okay Mom, I'll see you again and I love you.* "I love you Jolie," I sobbed. "Wait for me." I knew she would because animals don't reincarnate—they don't have to. They don't need to learn lessons of life like we do. They are just pure entities sent from God. I watched a white and condensed smokelike form leave her body and go straight across the room. The souls of animals don't have to go up because heaven (or the Other Side) is on this level, just in another dimension, with the same topography we have here except for the beautiful gardens, meadows, and temples. (We'll talk more about the Other Side later in this book.) In my psychic vision I could see Jolie romping through a garden of daffodils and playing and meeting my other dogs that had gone before. This gave me some small comfort, but as with all grief I felt cheated. I was glad she was happy, but selfishly I wanted her with me. Still, I knew she was happy, and I knew I'd see her again someday.

Our first teacher is our own heart.
—CHEYENNE

The hole our animals leave when they go is immeasurable, and even though life goes on (just as it does when any loved one leaves you), so many things remind you of them. No one meeting you at the door . . . the toys that are still around . . . even the empty food dishes seem like stark reminders of your missing friend. After Jolie passed, I just preferred to leave everything the way it was for awhile because honestly, I couldn't stand to get rid of the last vestiges of her. Yes, I did feel her around jumping on the bed and brushing against my leg, and several times I actually saw a little white blur in the backyard that I knew was my Jolie. But this loss hit me particularly hard, and I truly felt like just going to bed.

You don't, of course. You get up, you keep living your life, and when time goes by other dogs or pets take the place of your beloved pet. But no matter how much time goes by, that animal will always have a special place in your heart. Later on I'll share more of my own stories of pet love and loss, and you'll also read the remarkable stories of other people who have wondrous tales about their beloved pets, some poignant and sad, some inspiring in their bravery and protection, still others amazing tales of communication and love, but all of them truly moving and wondrous.

WHEN OUR PETS PERFORM EXTRAORDINARY ACTS

Presently I have four dogs, but when I was younger I had cats. Both types of animals have their own distinct personalities and I love each of them in their own special way. I have had so many dogs in my seventy-two years of life that it's hard to even remember all of the breeds— German shepherds, dachshunds, West Highland terriers, Rhodesian Ridgebacks,

Great Danes, Lhasa Apsos, Shar-Peis, Lab-radoodles, golden retrievers, Bijon Frises, Shih Tzus, English bulldogs, Labradors, Yorkshire terriers, not to mention a number of beloved mutts of mixed breeding—each one holding a special place in my heart, and each one with a distinct personality of their own. I still have some of my beloved dogs, but over the years I have lost many pets that were dear to me. The truth is, many times I've loved my animals more than some people in my life! An animal's loyalty is unfaltering, and a pet doesn't care how you look or what mood you're in; they just love you unconditionally, which we could all really learn from!

My dear grandmother (who was a psy-chic in her own right and very well known in Kansas City, Missouri) used to say if you find someone who doesn't like ani-mals, children, or music . . . run. Over all the years I have found this to be usually true, especially with those who don't like animals.

One amazing story my grandmother told me was an event her family wit-nessed secondhand, a tale that was told for years in their small community. My grandmother was born in Germany, but her family had made its way to the United States when she was very young, first to Texas and then to Springfield, Missouri, where the winters were horrendous. When I was a girl in that part of the world, we were literally snowbound for days at a time by the ferocity of winter storms (not anything like the milder winters experienced in that part of the world today, which as an aside supports the Greenhouse Theory!).

There was a family that lived next door to my grandmother's family, and they stepped out just a short distance away from home to get supplies one cold winter day and left their sleeping baby with their German shepherd, who really was like a watchful nanny to the baby. They intended to be gone just a few minutes, but while they were gone a sudden terrible snowstorm hit. It was the type of storm we used to call a whiteout—you literally couldn't see your hand in front of your face. After many hours the family finally made their way back to their house, and when they walked in, the baby's crib was empty. The house was freezing cold because the heat had dissipated in their absence. The German shepherd was cringing and whimpering under the bed. The husband in fear and dread deduced (as did the wife) that the dog had harmed the baby out of hunger or even fear of abandonment. The husband, out of his mind with grief, got his rifle and aimed it at the dog's head. Just as he cocked it to shoot they heard a faint cry. They looked under the bed and there was the baby cuddled up to the dog to keep it warm. The dog, realizing the peril of the baby possibly freezing to death, had lifted the baby and put it under the bed, wrapping its warm body around the child to keep it from freezing. My grandmother said the woman never quit talking about how horrible it would have been if they had killed the dog that saved their baby from freezing.

Now I know we can say the parents of the child were neglectful in leaving their baby in the care of their dog, but times then were different and much harder, and the sudden storm caught them unaware. But all that aside, consider the logical reasoning of this marvelous animal being. This wonderful dog knew, either instinctively or spiritually, how to save a human

being, realizing that if it were left in the freezing air the baby would have died.

That's why I know that dogs and other creatures are not just "dumb animals." They do think, feel, and sense. But are they directed by a "higher power" as some would say? I believe that, in the same way that our choices can be "directed" or influenced by God to help someone or save someone, so too can animals' behaviors be aimed toward good. We all are vessels of information infused from God, if we just listen, but an animal's brain doesn't have all the complexities that our mind does. Animals are just pure, uncomplicated entities of creation from God. They live like the Maasai do in Kenya—for each day is forever to them and the "Now" is what they live in. You can get aggravated with your pets and yell at them, but in a matter of minutes they are licking your hand again in love. Animals have no thoughts of vengeance and don't carry grudges; they are just simply loyal and loving creatures.

I don't think many people realize how sentient animals are. They can detect illness, for example. My friend had a black Labrador retriever, and every time he came up to her he literally would put his nose in her right eye and try to lick it. I watched this a few times and then I said, "Susan, just for the hell of it why don't you get an MRI, because that is not normal behavior." She finally did, and her doctor found a tumor just behind her right eye. Thankfully, the growth was caught in time, but the doctor said it could have spread and might have been very serious. Doctors are now finding that many dogs can not only smell drugs but can actually sniff out illness, especially tumors and cancer.

I have been privy to many such stories, and throughout this book I'll also tell you tales of animals who have gone to great lengths to protect and help the people they love—stories that are all part of our lives with these very spiritual beings we call our pets.

TAKING CARE OF
THE ANIMALS WE LOVE

There's no doubt that our animals are good to us; but sometimes we need to be reminded about how to treat them. Dr. Donald Coggans, who was the former Archbishop of Canterbury said: "Animals as part of God's Creation have rights which must be respected. It behooves us always to be sensitive to their needs and the reality of their pain." The famous Greek philosopher and mathematician Pythagoras stated: "As long as man continues to be a ruthless destroyer of lower living beings he will never know health or peace. For as long as man does needless massacre of animals they will kill each other. Indeed, he who sows the seeds of murder and pain cannot reap joy and love." According to the Bible, man has been given dominion over all living things. I believe in the end humankind will live to regret their abusive actions not only to animals but this planet we live on. It's interesting to note that every major religion puts forth in some way that animals should be loved and protected, yet we as animal lovers are still appalled by the cruelty that is heaped on them.

Animals never create wars, and wild animals only kill to survive. Wild animals, in particular, don't know avarice or vengeance, and even the ones that I have seen that seemed to go "mad" are usually influenced by some other forces, usually because man has either encroached on their territory or treated them in a brutal manner. It's not that they are vengeful in any way; they just want to survive and protect their young and territory. How many times have you seen on a nature program the disastrous effects of humankind's encroachment on the habitats of wild animals? The animals are only responding in a natural manner for their own survival. If we take away their natural prey due to our expansion on the land, then they in turn have to survive and begin to prey on domesticated animals or search for food in areas inhabited by man, which, of course, means that they will be hunted and killed because they are considered a danger or nuisance. They are only trying to survive, but humankind, as it always has, will continue to kill and expand and exterminate species after species.

Finally, in this book, we'll look at ways we can protect the animals we love—both those we keep as pets and the majestic beasts in the wild—and how we can each act as a steward and friend to the creatures we love most.

Some people may find it offensive when I say I prefer my pets to some people I've met—the truth is, they are more loving, loyal, compassionate, and, yes, even smarter in some instances! But as I always say in all my writings—take with you what you want and leave the rest. One fact I'm sure of is that God created animals not just to feed and clothe us but to be our loving companions in life that comfort, protect, and warn us, as well as understand more than we ever think they do.

Whether you are a pet owner or not, animals *do* affect your life—it's just that with pet owners, animals affect our lives in a much greater sense than those who don't own pets. Not only do animals help to clothe and feed us, but depending upon the pet and the family, our relationship with an animal can be as close as or closer than with any human being. Throughout this book we'll look at the special bonds between humans and animals. But it's important to remember that this close relationship is not a new phenomenon; humans have revered animals for centuries. So before we get into modern tales of human/animal companionship and respect, we'll first look back at the important roles that animals have played in the lives of people for millennia.

Regard Heaven as your Father, Earth as your Mother and all things as your Brothers and Sisters.
—TRIBE UNKNOWN

2

ANIMALS IN THE LIVES OF
THE ANCIENTS

"Man's law changes with his understanding of man.
Only the laws of the spirit remain
always the same."
—**Crow Indian proverb**

Today, it's easy to see the prominent role
that animals play in our lives—in fact, many
people would say they "worship" their pets
and would do anything to protect them.
And it's true that people today have more
money and resources to spend on their
animals than ever before. But as you'll see
in this chapter, animals have always held
a prominent role in the lives of the humans
who love them. Our reverence for our pets
is nothing new, and we've always recognized the special and spiritual qualities in
the animals that are close to us.

In the United States alone, there are over 160 million pets at last count, which comes out to be a little over one pet for every two people. More than $24 billion was spent in 2007 for veterinary services alone, and more than $47 billion for veterinary services and products combined— all for our beloved pets. A recent American Veterinary Medical Association survey has approximately 60 percent of American families and singles owning pets. Two-thirds of pet-owning households have more than one pet, and 20 percent of pet-owning households have at least five pets. Needless to say, pets are an important part of the lives of many Americans, and I'm sure this trend will continue more or less throughout the world.

The increased amount of money spent on pet care has resulted in longer lives for our pets. The above survey says that in 2007, 44 percent of dogs were more than six years old, while in 1987, only 32 percent were older than six. It is the same with cats—44 percent of cats in 2007 were more than six years old, and in 1987 only 28 percent were older than six. Veterinarians say that's due in large part to the fact that pet owners are spending more on the health problems of their pets, and treating diseases such as cancer, diabetes, and heart disease (they even put pacemakers in animals now!) rather than just having their pets euthanized. It seems that pet owners are becoming closer to their pets emotionally, and in fact 48.7 percent of pet owners consider their pets to be "part of their family," according to a survey recently put out by the U.S. Consumer Bureau.

Tell me and I'll forget. Show me, and I may not remember. Involve me, and I'll understand.
—TRIBE UNKNOWN

The increased attention to their pets by pet owners is not without its own controversy, however. Many who don't own pets or do not have a close emotional bond with animals point out that the money spent on pets would be better spent taking care of adults and children who need food, clothing, health care, housing, and so on. They essentially argue that human beings are more important than animals, which I'm sure could be debated from now until doomsday. An animal lover could simply argue that there is more money spent on luxury items than for animals, so forgo that luxury car, boat, airplane, and house and give the money to charities that take care of human beings.

Those of us who have pets generally love them to varying degrees, and also take care of them in different ways. Essentially you can put pet owners into one of four categories—excellent, good, fair, and bad or abusive.

The excellent pet owner absolutely adores and loves his pets and will do anything for them. This pet owner has made an absolute bond with his or her pets that many times supersedes even human relationships, and these types of owners can treat their pets like human beings. This category of pet owner generally considers his pets to be part of his family, and because they are animal lovers they usually have more than one pet. They also tend to spend more money on their pets and on health care for their pets.

The good pet owner is probably the category under which most pet owners fall.

The good owners treat their pets kindly and give them varying amounts of attention and love and may or may not consider them to be part of the family. This category of pet owner also includes the majority of families that have children. Typically because the family does have children, pets may not get the attention and devotion that the excellent pet owner gives, simply because there is not as much to go around after the children get their rightful share.

The fair pet owner is generally one that doesn't necessarily give a lot of attention or love to their pets, but does make sure that they are properly fed and basically taken care of. You will find this owner many times to be one who has animals as service or working animals as well as pets. Their pets may work for their room and board, so to speak. You will also find that this owner has too many things going on in his life to give much time or attention to his pet, and usually his pet is not an indoor pet. These pet owners may like animals but aren't necessarily big animal lovers. This type of owner also will give his pet away or give him to the pound if the pet becomes too much of an inconvenience in his life. Generally speaking, this type of owner should not have pets because he doesn't give them the love and attention that they should have, and the only thing that saves him from being a bad owner is that he does feed and care for them minimally well.

The bad pet owner is just that—not only a bad owner but a bad human being. These pet owners give their pets practically no attention or love and, in fact, many times will beat and abuse them unmercifully. This type of owner will also translate that abuse into their own lives and many times will be involved in alcohol or drug abuse, unlawful activities, and perhaps into child and spousal abuse. This is the owner that will starve or neglect his animals or even train them to fight for pleasure or profit.

When you see news clips on television showing starving or abused animals, this is the type of owner that owns these animals. If you are ever a witness to this kind of cruelty to animals, please report the people responsible to the local law enforcement authorities. If it is someone you

know, you can always report them anony-
mously.

Sharing and giving are the ways
of God.
—SAUK

As animals take up a big part of the
lives of most people, it is only natural that
we want to know more about them, which
is why we have so many television programs about animals and even complete
television channels such as *Animal Planet*
devoted to them. But this close relationship between animals and humans isn't
a new phenomenon; humans have had a
close relationship with the animals they love
since the time of the ancients. We are now
going to explore the origins of this special
bond between animals and humans.

The Origins of Domesticated Animals

Dogs as a species are thought by scientists to have evolved from wolves. The
domestication of animals as well as plants
evolved over long periods of time. Most

scientists think that dogs were the first animals to be domesticated, and some put their domestication as far back as 15,000 BCE. Scientists say the domestication process began either with natural selection or with selected breeding, a debate that goes on even today. In natural selection the wild animal mutates outside of human control to a form that is more conducive to human domestication. An example of this might be wolves coming closer to humans and living off their scraps, and over generations becoming smaller and less ferocious due to human contact and less hunting and more scavenging. In selected breeding, however, early man would capture animals (in this case wolves) that seemed to be less antagonistic and breed them, and over time their offspring would become much tamer in disposition. In truth, scientists suspect the actual method of domestication was probably some combination of these two methods. Regardless of the process used, the outcome was that early man over the course of time turned wolves into the domesticated animal we know today as the dog.

In Russia an experiment was done by the Russian scientist Dmitri Belyaev in the 1950s with silver foxes to prove selected breeding as a means of domestication. His team of researchers spent quite a few years breeding captive wild silver foxes. They only selected foxes that showed the least fear of humans, and out of those, they selected the foxes that seemed to interact with humans better than others. After several generations of breeding the results were astounding. Not only did their appearance change with rolled tails, smaller heads, and floppy ears which are common traits in many dogs today, but their behavior changed dramatically, to the point where they showed no fear of humans, often wagged their tails, and would lick and show affection to their caretakers.

Many of the first domesticated dogs were called "protodogs" by scientists, and many were found buried along with their masters in ancient tombs. Many cave drawings show dogs helping ancient men in the hunt, and because of their enhanced senses of hearing and smell and their barking, dogs were also used as protectors in their various camps to warn of possible encroaching dangers.

Look at the German shepherd's head and body and you can see the resemblance to its wolf ancestors. Scientists believe that over the millennia early dogs not only mutated because of captivity but were bred for certain characteristics, which has led to the many different breeds of dogs that we have today. For example, the malamute and husky were bred for pulling sleds with loads in the northern climates of snow and ice, and their thick coats protect them from the freezing weather. In contrast, Lhasa Apsos are tiny dogs that were bred more for their pleasing looks, even though they and Shiatsus were used as guard dogs for Chinese temples and palaces. You might wonder how such small dogs could be guard dogs, but the keen senses of dogs and their ability to bark makes any dog a watchdog. It has been shown that a barking dog is more of a deterrent to intruders than any expensive protection device or alarm system. Scientists believe that they are protective because they are very territorial, and this transcends over centuries to their protecting us, not discounting their ability to sense, hear, and smell what we cannot.

In ancient Egypt dogs and cats were buried in tombs with their owners. Cats were particularly popular in ancient Egypt because they disposed of various vermin and also became household pets. Dogs were used for protection and also became pets, but not on as large a scale as cats. Cats were more likely put in tombs because they were pets and because the ancient Egyptians also worshipped the cat goddess Bast. Dogs were mummified and buried in tombs also as pets, but more for protection to guard the spirit of their owner in the perils of the journey to the afterlife.

Scientists believe that geography and environment also had a huge hand in developing domesticated dogs from wolves. Different types of wolves were indigenous to certain areas, and the harsher the climate or environment the stronger the line of wolves. Nature has its own way of making sure only the strong and hardy survive. Scientists use an amazing database from every part of the world to follow the evolution of animals just like they do with people. They found that different animals

survived better in different climates and areas than others, and this was particularly the case with dogs. As people migrated and traveled the world, the onset of different breeds of dogs took place, and breeding was adapted to whatever climate or area they were in, as well as the type of work they wanted the dog to do. What would the Inuit (Eskimos) do without their sled dogs or the sheep farmers do without their sheepdogs? Interestingly enough, sheep and goats were thought to be the next in line as far as domestication was concerned, and man is thought to have domesticated them along with the pig and cat between 11,000 and 9,000 BCE, but the dog predated all these other species in domestication by almost four thousand years!

As ancient man moved from becoming

strictly a hunter-gatherer to becoming more agriculturally orientated, more and more animals were domesticated either for food, clothing, or work. Sheep, pigs, and goats were the first animals raised for food and clothing, and then came the cow, which was domesticated in India, Africa, and the Middle East around 8,000 BCE. Two thousand years later the chicken was domesticated in India and Southeast Asia around 6,000 BCE. Over the next several thousand years we see that many of the working animals were domesticated such as the donkey (Egypt—5,000 BCE), water buffalo (India, China—4,000 BCE), camel (Arabia—4,000 BCE), horse (Central Asia—4,000 BCE), and llama (Peru—3,500 BCE). These animals helped not only in the raising of crops but also in establishing numerous trade routes in the ancient world. It's truly a fact that God gave us these different animals to help us in our development and everyday life.

Native American tribes loved and worshipped animals for giving them food and clothing, and my spirit guide Francine says they always had dogs around their camps to warn of danger and also to be companions to them. They would even warn them if there was a marauding tribe nearby.

When I was in Kenya, the Kikuyu, Maasai, and Samburu tribes also had dogs to warn them of wild animals that were around. In fact, the Rhodesian Ridgeback came originally from South Africa when the Dutch bred their dogs with the semiwild ridged hunting dogs of the Khoisan tribe, which were referred to as Hottentots by the Dutch settlers and colonists. The Rhodesian Ridgeback is known for a ridge of hair along its back that grows in the opposite direction. They have also been called the African Lion Hound or African Lion Dog for their ability to harass lions and keep them at bay until their masters would arrive. The reason I mention these dogs is because I actually had a pair of Rhodesian Ridgebacks and I named the male Bear and the female Simba. Shortly thereafter I was blessed (I think) with nine puppies, and they were a handful until I was able to sell or give them away. In spite of their reputation as lion hunters and a dog that should be handled only by experienced dog owners, I found them to be kind dogs to my family and children. They do tend to be standoffish with strangers. Like many dogs whose loyalty is immeasurable, Rhodesians seem to go far beyond any dog I've had. When they want your attention they put their paws on your feet as if to say "notice me!"

When I was growing up we had cats as pets and I loved them also. I loved their warmth, as they sat or lay on your lap, the sound of their purring, but my preference is dogs. Both have psychic ability, especially cats. That's one reason why in ancient times they condemned cats as familiars to witches, which meant the person thought to be a witch could change herself into a cat or command a cat to do her bidding. This is all legend, of course, but cats are more known for their independence, cunning, and stealth like all the cats in the wild today. Domesticated cats are only utilized as pets today and although they may catch the occasional rat or mouse, in ancient times cats were used in great numbers to control vermin problems as you will see a bit later on.

Interestingly, cats today seem to be the preferred pet of females more than males, and conversely dogs seem to be preferred by more males than females as pets, though there are certainly many exceptions to this!

It may well be just that cats have always been associated with the feminine such as the cat goddess Bast or witches or just society in general. When we say someone is being "catty" it always refers to a female. On the other hand, cats seem to be much more fastidious than dogs as they are constantly cleaning themselves and will go to the bathroom in their litter box while a dog has to be taken outside and will go in any number of places. Dogs have always been associated with the outdoors, which has also been termed the domain of men, and cats are more indoor pets, a realm that has always been associated with women. Cats also make excellent pets for confined spaces such as apartments, while dogs like to roam over larger areas. Both cats and dogs today are mostly adored as pets, and many families have both and they get along just like other members of the family.

To touch the earth is to have harmony with nature.
—OGLALA SIOUX

From all that scientists and historians can gather it seems that the first "gods" all came from nature and this includes animals. In fact, most scientists agree that aside from the Sun, Moon, Stars, Wind, Rain, Fire, and so on the first gods or deities took the form of animals. They, like me, would logically assume that early man worshipped animals because many had more power, strength, and speed than early human beings. Many an early human was probably injured or killed by some animal, and they not only gained the respect of humans at that time but were in all probability feared or worshipped because they were more powerful. Early prehistoric cave drawings show many more animals than human beings, and some of these caves became shrines of worship.

One of the earliest was a shrine devoted to the Cave Bear in a cave in the Swiss Alps called "Drachenloch" (Cave of the Dragons). This particular cave was at an altitude of approximately eight thousand feet and was discovered and excavated by the German archaeologist Emil Bachler from 1917 to 1923. His conclusions were that the site was from seventy-five thousand to eighty thousand years old and was one of the earliest Neanderthal habitats discovered up to that time. The cave was quite large with the area closest to the entrance having substantial evidence of habitation by Neanderthal man. Farther back in the cave, a primitive altar was discovered that had a half dozen or so bear skulls inside, all pointing toward the entrance as if to guard or provide protection, and further back another twenty or so bear skulls were found individually in niches in the cave walls. This discovery was one of the earliest indicating animal worship ever found.

Another interesting thing is that animals seem to dominate in the stories and myths that were handed down through the generations of early man and even to this day in the tales of Native Americans; their heroes are generally not people but animals or stars. Animal deities were predominant in early man's world. In very ancient times, as the environment changed and species such as the mammoth and saber-toothed tiger became extinct, early man only had the memories of these powerful beasts in his oral tradition. As time went on, the worship of these animals ceased and the worship of new animals came into being. As certain animal deities died out, new deities of the animals around them came into being, and ancient man eventually gave more and more attributes to them.

Ancient man observed what went on around him and was a slave to his senses. Lightning and volcanoes gave fire, lakes and rivers and streams and rain gave water, certain animals gave clothing and hides for warmth and shelter, and all of these circumstances led to pantheistic religions over time.

As early man evolved further and moved from the hunter to the farmer, so did the animal deities evolve. If a particular culture was more hunter oriented, animal deities remained strong, but if the culture was more agriculturally disposed, animal deities started giving way to anthropomorphic ones (deities with human characteristics) in the form of goddesses. As I basically explained in my book *Mother God*, the goddess as a deity came into being before her male counterpart in most cultures due to the advent of agriculture. The human female is the one who carries and births children and as such became the symbol of fertility. Animal deities became fewer and fewer in number, and over the years the traits of the animal were transferred to the human goddess or god, and the animal deities were thereby assimilated into the various anthropomorphic religions.

One of the earliest examples of this was found in one of my favorite places, the Anatolia region in Turkey. Excavations conducted at Catal Huyuk found that the earliest shrines were to animals—namely the bull. They then found the first shrines to a goddess, dated to approximately 6,200 BCE, which reflected the change from a hunting to an agricultural society and also showed the esteem in which women were held. Most scientists believe that the switch from the goddess to the male god took place with the urbanization of society. As cities came into being and more people were gathered in one place, the male god seemed to take precedence and came more and more into power.

The animal deities died hard, however, and the traits of animals persisted in many of the gods of these ancient civilizations. Athena with the owl, Zeus with the eagle, and Aphrodite with the dove are just a few examples of how animals still held some tenure in religions. There are still animal deities in existence today, and ancient man either assimilated these deities into his new religions or coexisted with them. Even in modern-day religions we still see the influence of these animal deities as the Hindus have Ganesha, the elephant-headed god of wisdom; the Buddhists have Wu-Kung, the monkey fairy who attained enlightenment; the dove represents the Holy Spirit in Christianity; and all of the major religions are rich in animal symbolism.

All of the ancient religions have stories of the gods utilizing animals or taking animal forms, such as the story of Zeus, who seduced various women in the form of a swan or a bull (that must have hurt); many of early man's heroes were either aided by or took the form of an animal to vanquish various monsters or rescue some princess or other. Fairy tales and myths are filled with animals that talk, aid, or give wisdom as supposedly do many of the ancient animal deities. From the days of ancient Egypt, Greece, Rome, and the Americas, animals have always played a crucial role in the lives of humans. So that we can better understand the spiritual lives of the animals we love today, let's first take a look back at the role animals have played in our lives since the earliest days of written history.

What is life? It is the flash of a firefly in the night. It is the breath of a buffalo in the wintertime. It is the little shadow which runs across the grass and loses itself in the sunset.
—BLACKFOOT

Animal Worship in Ancient Egypt

Contrary to what many popularly believe, religion in ancient Egypt was not very unified and did not just consist of worshipping the Pharaoh as a god. In fact, there was a potpourri of unsystematic beliefs and practices that could vary by region or even social class. Depending upon the time and place, animals could depict characteristics of the gods, such as Horus having his falcon head because he was believed to have falconlike qualities and the goddess Bast (also called Bastet) being depicted as a cat and linked to fertility and child rearing. Thoth, the divine scribe of the gods, had the head of an ibis and was an object of worship for having great learning and wisdom. The jackal-headed god Anubis was the god of embalming and the mummified dead and set the balance in the weighing of hearts. The goddess Maat had the ostrich feather as her emblem and it was the weight against which a person's heart was measured after death. Hathor, the great Egyptian goddess of motherhood, fertility, and love, was depicted as having either a cow's head, or as having a cow's horns and a solar disk on her head.

The above deities were what we might consider the major gods along with Isis, Osiris, Ptah, and the great sun god Re (also called Ra), but there were also many other gods and goddesses that were more minor in nature or served certain local areas of Egypt.

There were also a plethora of household gods who watched over the home and family that were mainly for the lower classes, while the Pharaoh and the wealthy upper classes celebrated the major gods and goddesses that were also celebrated nationally at least once a year. Almost all of the gods, whether for the lower or higher classes, had some attribute of an animal attached to them.

As Egypt's civilization evolved, some of these gods or goddesses evolved into what we might call animal cults, and the actual animal associated with the deity became an object of worship. One of the deities worshipped by Egyptians was known as the Apis Bull, which was considered to house the god Ptah. Ptah was the god of craftsmen and artisans, but also was considered the creator of the world. There was only one Apis Bull at a time, and he supposedly had special markings that signified him as the holy receptacle of the god Ptah. The live bull was treated like a god; it had its own bevy of priests and was housed at Ptah's own temple in Memphis. The head priest at the temple was charged with being able to read various movements and actions of the bull to foresee the future and answer the questions of various worshippers. Lesser priests were charged with the care of the bull and taking in the various offerings that were offered by the populace. When any Apis Bull died, a search was immediately started by the priests for another bull that had the necessary holy markings, and the dead bull was mummified and buried with great ceremony in its own tomb.

While the Apis Bull cult following was large, it did not compare with the eventual popularity of the animal cult formed for the goddess Bast. Bast or Bastet as mentioned earlier was represented by a cat—she was the goddess of child rearing and fertility, and either had the head of a cat or was depicted as a cat herself. The Bast cult came into the height of its popularity about two thousand to three thousand years ago, and really represented the elevated place that cats held in Egyptian society.

Ancient Egypt was very good at the domestication of animals in general, and this was especially true as far as the wild cat was concerned. The wild jungle cat and the African wildcat were the two types of cats that were basically native to Egypt. Larger than the average house cat today, they were quite fierce and very good at killing poisonous snakes (even cobras), and even more important the various mice, rats, and other vermin that would eat the grains of the royal granaries. The African wildcat had a better temperament, and most of the cats that were eventually domesticated came from that species and evolved over the years to what we now know as the Egyptian Mau.

Because of their value in the killing of various vermin, cats were quickly domesticated, and almost every temple and certainly every granary had at least several cats in residence to control the various pests. In the temples to Bast, priests had anywhere from a few dozen to hundreds of cats in residence that they would take care of. With their great ability to reproduce in large numbers, cats soon became a fixture in almost every city, town, or village in Egypt. Many were house pets, many were installed in temples, and many just roamed the streets.

As the popularity of cats grew, they became more and more sacred to the ancient Egyptians. They not only controlled the vermin populations but made nice pets for the household. Out of the popularity for cats, the popularity of the goddess Bast also grew and soon cats also caused another by-product, a growing revenue source. The mummification of cats became more popular as many mummified cats were offered to the goddess Bast in addition to money and food. Scientists say the mummification of animals became big business and various animals were mummified for three basic reasons—as offerings to various gods, as a food source for a mummified human being to eat on his journey in the afterlife, and because they were beloved pets and the owner hoped to take them along into the afterlife.

The mummification of the dead was already a big business in ancient Egypt, but when the mummification of animals became popular the business of mummification became even larger. Priests or people would raise animals (mainly cats) for the express purpose of killing them, mummifying them, and selling them to those who wanted to offer them to the various gods. In addition, artisans were called upon for more statues of these gods, especially for those of the goddess Bast. This created a number of sidelines of business all related to the religious worship of gods, and increased revenues in the form of taxes for the Pharaoh.

As animals became more sacred, laws were enacted for their protection. The Greek historian Herodotus stated that anyone in ancient Egypt who intentionally killed a sacred animal was put to death. Diodorus, another Greek historian, said that a Roman citizen whose chariot accidentally killed a cat was lynched by an Egyptian mob even though the Pharaoh tried to intervene on his behalf.

The mummification of animals shows the high regard the ancient Egyptians had for them, and although mummified animals have been found in various tombs of human beings, the high degree of mummification of animals is mostly shown in the huge repositories that have been found in the areas of Bubastis, Saqqara, Thebes, and Beni Hasan. In these locales huge "tombs" of mummified animals were mostly cats; the tomb outside Beni Hasan alone held more than nineteen tons of mummified animals remains.

The cult of Bast came to an end when it was officially banned by imperial decree in AD 390. Under the rule of ancient Rome,

all of the beliefs in the ancient gods went into a marked decline and were effectively stamped out. Today in modern Egypt cats are still kept as pets and tolerated elsewhere, but there is now no religious significance attached to them.

ANIMAL WORSHIP IN ANCIENT GREECE AND ROME

In ancient Rome the earliest religion was ancestor worship, but Rome became very eclectic as its empire became more powerful. Nowhere is this more evident than in the Romans literally taking the ancient gods of Greece as their own. The Romans simply gave the bulk of Greek gods new names—thus Zeus became Jupiter, Hera became Juno, Poseidon became Neptune, and so on, and Rome also incorporated all of Greek mythology as part of its religion with few changes.

The ancient gods of Greece are perhaps the most fascinating of all the ancient civilizations because their influence and mythology still affect us today. It isn't that their gods were more powerful, but we can certainly say they were more colorful in nature because of the many human attributes given to them. In addition to having the human frailties of emotion, such as anger, love, revenge, and so on, it is probably the stories about these gods that has made them endure and remain in the consciousness of humankind over the ages. All people love a good story or epic, and the ancient Greeks had them in abundance when it came to their gods—from the many stories about Zeus and his seducing various females in different animal or human forms to the fabulous feats and adventures of the mighty hero Hercules. With this in mind, did animals take any major role in the ancient Greek religion?

Much like the ancient Egyptian religion, certain Greek deities were associated with certain animals or their traits. We have Zeus associated with the eagle (power),

Athena with the owl (wisdom), Hermes has his wings (speed), but except for the Greek gods Dionysus (who many believed took the form of a goat) or Poseidon (who took the form of half man and fish), the Greeks reference to animals in their religion is mainly that of mythological creatures. Whether the mythological creature was a feared enemy to some hero such as Medusa, the Cyclops, or the Cretan Bull or a helpful animal such as Pegasus was to Perseus, animals do play an extensive part in the mythology of Greece.

One of the few Greek animal cults that were known to have existed is that of the snake god Glycon. This cult was supposedly founded by the Greek prophet Alexander of Abonutichus and probably originated in Macedonia where minor snake cults had existed for centuries, as the Greeks believed snakes had magical powers relating to fertility. Greek mythology had a rich history on the subject of snakes, and the prime example is when Zeus impregnated Olympia disguised as a serpent. Supposedly the cult of Glycon initially worshipped a real serpent, which again, supposedly, embodied the reincarnated god Asclepius (Greek god of medicine and healing). Alexander had evidently foretold that Asclepius would take on a new incarnation, and at the appointed time, he withdrew a serpent egg and sliced it open. It was said that within a week the serpent grew to the size of a man and had the features of a human face with long blond hair. Historians believe that when the god Glycon appeared in the temple it was either a puppet or a trained serpent upon which was placed a puppet head to look like a human face. Although the main focus of worship to Glycon was fertility (women would bring offerings in the hope of bearing a child), Glycon was also thought by many to offer protection against plague.

One of the more interesting mythological characters in Greek mythology was the centaur—in particular one centaur named Chiron. Centaurs were creatures that had the form of half horse and half man and had the reputation for constantly drinking and carousing, becoming angry when drunk, and were generally thought to be uncivilized. Chiron, although a centaur, was completely different from other centaurs and was said to be immortal because he was born from the union of the Titan Cronus and the nymph Phillyra when Cronus took the form of a horse in her seduction. Chiron was intelligent, kind, wise, and a great teacher of the healing arts and the lyre. He basically raised both Achilles and Jason who became famous Greek heroes. He also became the mentor of Asclepius, to whom he taught the healing arts, and of Theseus, another hero who killed the Minotaur and rescued captives from its maze. Chiron was accidentally hit by a poisoned arrow from Hercules and, at the request of Hercules, gave up his immortality because he was in great pain and gave it to Prometheus, after Hercules had freed him from his captivity by Zeus.

Thus we can see that the religion of Greece was filled with gods in abundance as well as monsters, mythological beasts, and animals. When the Roman Empire came to its full glory the assimilation of the Greek gods was already complete. The Romans also assimilated the goddess Isis as well as the god Mithras from other ancient religions. All of these gods were finally done away with when the emperor Constantine made the Christian faith the state religion of Rome.

**Force, no matter how concealed,
begets resistance.**
—LAKOTA

ANIMAL WORSHIP IN
THE ANCIENT AMERICAS

Archaeology as a science is one of the most enlightening tools that humankind has for exploring our past. Like all sciences its beliefs are ever changing because new sites or information are found constantly, which challenge the beliefs that science in general has put forth previously. We can truly say that science in its own way is forever Gnostic in nature because it is constantly seeking the truth in new theories, thoughts, and ideas. It is sometimes its own worst enemy in that new theories or beliefs are almost always challenged, but unlike religion science will change its belief system when truth presents itself and is not as bogged down as religion because of long-standing tradition. It is true that science is sometimes slow to change, but it does eventually change, which is more than organized religion can claim.

Recent archaeological digs in Peru have uncovered what is believed to be the oldest "civilization" in the Americas, which is called the Caral Supe Civilization. The news about this find first came out in 2001, and carbon dating on archaeological objects found there date this civilization to about 2,600 BCE. This may change in the near future, because the archaeologists have not carbon dated the oldest of the sites yet, and there has been another find apart from this area that purportedly shows engineered canals that predate the Caral Supe site. I am sure that within the next few years more information about these sites will come forth.

The reason I bring this subject up is because for many years scientists have always thought that the cradle of civilization was either in Africa or in the Mesopotamia region. These recent finds in South America are slowly bringing the civilizations in the Americas closer to being contemporary with early civilizations in Mesopotamia. The earliest known permanent settlement in the Americas is that of the Valdivia on the coast of Ecuador, which dates to 3,500 BCE.

The problem has always been one of definition. Just what attributes are needed to classify a certain people as a "civilization"? Just what distinguishes uncivilized "savages" from those that are supposedly civilized? Scientists say it is order in the form of social structures, government, and public works, but that kind of definition will always be disputed. I personally feel that other than Atlantis and Lemuria, the first "civilizations" probably were in India and possibly China. Recent archaeological finds in India have been found to be dated to 9,500 BCE and many think they may be much older.

Now, what has this to do with ancient deities in the Americas? India and China are perhaps the most advanced cultures in the world today that believe in *animism.* Animism is in all religions today in different forms, but basically defined it is the belief in the soul and that souls occupy not only the human body but other forms of creation such as animals, plants, and even inanimate objects such as mountains. Although the major religions of Christianity, Judaism, and Islam only believe a soul occupies the human body, they still practice a form of animism. Most people acknowledge, however, that the practice of animism as it should be defined incorporates not only the human soul but that of other living and inanimate objects having souls. It is this definition of animism that was fully believed in the ancient cultures and civilizations of the Americas.

The oldest known deity in the Americas is simply called the "Staff God," because although it is called by different names depending upon the civilization, all the major civilizations depict this deity with the body of a human, fangs coming from the mouth with claws for feet and hands and holding a staff in each (although some depictions have one hand ending in a serpent). It is indigenous to South America, Mexico, and the Yucatán Peninsula and was a deity in all the major civilizations of that area, which included the Olmecs, Toltecs, Maya, Aztec, Inca, and even the newly discovered Caral

Supe. This deity has both human and animal characteristics, which in many cultures is not uncommon.

The most worshipped animal for all of the above religions was the jaguar. This would not be uncommon because most animal deities that were worshipped were those that humans interacted with in everyday life. The jaguar occupies Mexico, the Yucatán, and South America and was considered to be a deity because of its strength and craftiness in hunting prowess in either day or night. Killing a jaguar could result in a death penalty in some cultures, while in others the skin of the jaguar could only be worn by royalty or those held in high esteem. Snakes and birds were also held in high esteem and worshipped, and the Aztec worshipped as one of their three high gods the feathered serpent god named Quetzalcoatl.

In North America animism was practiced almost universally by the various Native American tribes from the Inuit (Eskimo) in Alaska to the Navajo and Hopi of the Southwest to the Iroquois Nation in the Northeast to the Cherokee and Seminole in the Southeast. The diversity of these tribes in their various beliefs and religions could take up volumes, but all practiced animism in one form or another. Contrary to widespread thinking, almost all tribes had either a monotheistic god or a god of duality. The Iroquois were perhaps the most monotheistic and they referred to their god as The Great Spirit. They also are considered by historians to have been the easiest to assimilate into Christian society in early America, probably due to their monotheistic leanings which also reflect those of Christianity.

Most religions of the Native Americans are directly linked to their respect for nature and keeping it in balance. Native American societies were either based on hunting or agriculture, and much of their individual beliefs in religion reflect these two modes of survival. The Plains tribes gave great credence and worship to the buffalo, and were nomadic because they followed the buffalo for food and clothing. Other hunter tribes like the Inuit and the Apache had a much harder time in hunting their food due to the extremes of their environments—cold and ice in Alaska and Canada and the arid deserts of Arizona and northern Mexico. Some tribes such as the Iroquois had the best of both worlds. They had lands that had an abundance of game and fish, which could also be sown with crops. That gave them more diversity and plenty as a people.

Maintaining a balance in nature was one of the priorities of the Native Americans, as it was nature that provided for them. Whether it was a hunter who gave homage to the soul of a slain animal by ritual so that the soul would encourage others of his kind to be killed as necessary, or the ritual dances and sacred drums and chants that were used for rain and fertility in the sowing of crops, Native Americans not only respected nature but also gave it homage for providing them with food and the means for survival.

Nearly all Native Americans used animism in their various religious practices. Animals had souls or spirits as did aspects of Mother Nature such as rain, storms, thunder, lightning, the sun and moon and stars. Certain places also had spirits and were considered sacred such as particular mountains or valleys or rivers or lakes.

The creation myths and other mythologies of the various tribes were all handed down orally by elders or medicine men or shamans. Native Americans viewed the world as either unchangeable and thus to be respected and kept in balance or as a world that had a unity with a supernatural world of spirits, and again harmony had to be maintained between both. It is perhaps this unity in trying to maintain balance and harmony that has led me to believe that Native American culture is one of the most spiritual in the world today.

Animals and the forces of nature are acknowledged and respected and sometimes deified because of their importance in everyday life. The spirit world is respected and known to exist to either help or hinder, depending upon the actions of the individual or tribe. Many tribes put more emphasis on individual spiritual experiences to find one's place in life, and many have rituals that encourage these spiritual experiences not only to better the individual but also to help and guide the tribe in general.

Much of what we know about Native

Americans has been generated by the white man, and I've always said history is written by the winners. So much of Native American culture has been lost because of the lack of a written language, as their culture was handed down orally for centuries before the white man invaded their shores. In the course of three to four hundred years the culture and population of the Native American were almost wiped out completely from the face of the earth. Driven from their lands in the name of progress for natural resources or development, they now live on designated reservations. Human rights abuses by our government against them still take place today, such as the desecration of sacred sites. It is sad how so-called "civilization" has literally wiped out so many cultures that are deemed "heathen" or "savage" but are instead many times more spiritual than our own. The wisdom and proverbs of the Native Americans show this great spirituality, which is why I've included some of them in this book. Their culture also reflects perhaps more than any other their respect and love of animals.

We are all one child spinning through Mother Sky.
—SHAWNEE

ANIMALS IN RELIGIONS TODAY

In most if not all modern religions there are no animal deities. Some early forms of modern-day religion have used animals as sacrifices, such as in the early days of Judaism, when animals (mostly sheep or goats or birds) were sacrificed on altars, but the practice does not take place today to any extent.

Christianity for the most part believes that animals are beneath humans in the scope of creation, as written in the Book of Genesis in the Bible where God puts animals under the dominion of men. The Book of Genesis (being Judaic in origin) also has the same influence on modern-day Judaism so the belief that animals are below humans is the most prevalent in that religion, too. The religion of Islam views animals as a special part of God's creation and generally extols kindness to animals, but like Judaism and Christianity animals are not considered to be the equal of humankind. Interestingly, all three of these major religions have followers who eat the meat of animals and some hunt them for sport.

It is in the major Eastern religions that animals seem to be on a more equal footing with humankind in creation. Contrary to popular belief, in the religion of Hinduism animals are not worshipped. Hinduism believes in a certain form of reincarnation that entails "the transmigration of souls," which basically means that if a person incurs bad karma in his life due to bad deeds and actions, he may be incarnated in the body of an animal in their next life. Thus, Hindus believe that all animals can contain the soul of a human being, and since their religion is so pacifistic in nature they espouse no harm be given to any living creature. That is the reason why you can see cows wandering freely around and even a temple dedicated to feeding and taking care of rats. At the rat temple people eat the same food that is given to the rats—and many times off the same plate.

These animals are not being worshipped; they are being taken care of by the general populace so they will not starve, suffer, or die.

I respect the Hindu religion's love of animals, but from all my research I haven't personally ever found anything that would make me believe in transmigration. I believe in reincarnation, but I do not believe in the transmigration of souls. My guide Francine has always said that humans do reincarnate, but only as human beings. Actually much of the belief in karma and transmigration of souls came from the ancient caste system, which supposedly has been refuted by law but is still practiced today. If a soul lived a good life he or she would incarnate in a higher caste in the next life, and conversely if a soul lived a bad life he or she would incarnate in a lower caste or even lower into an animal. That being said, I still find the Hindu faith very beautiful in many ways and certainly respect it as one of the major religions of humankind.

Some Hindu deities have portions of their bodies in animal form. For instance, Ganesha, one of the five prime Hindu deities, has the head of an elephant on a human body with four arms. The elephant head is symbolic as Ganesha is considered the Lord of Success, the destroyer of evils and obstacles, and is the deity of education, knowledge, wisdom, and wealth. The Hindu religion purportedly has over thirty thousand deities, many of which are local to a certain area and are only deified by small segments of Hindus.

Hinduism has always practiced Ahimsa (the law of noninjury and nonharming), and it is considered a Hindu's first duty in fulfilling their religious practices to God and Creation and is defined in Vedic scripture. For instance, in Yajur Veda (12.32) it states: *You must not use your God-given body for killing God's creatures, whether they are human, animal or whatever.* It is not surprising that almost all Hindus are vegetarians.

Sikhism and Buddhism both evolved out of Hinduism and have similar values in regard to animals or any living being. Sikhs initiated into the Khalsa Brotherhood eat no meat, eggs, or fish, although Sikhs not practicing the Khalsa code of conduct may eat meat. Most Sikhs, however, are vegetarian. In Buddhism one of the central tenets is to not harm any living being. Buddha himself was not a vegetarian and purportedly ate meat from time to time. He supposedly advised that meat should only be eaten if one knew the animal had not been killed specifically for oneself. Thus, meat in grocery stores is acceptable to eat because it was not killed specifically for one person. Some Buddhists eat meat, but the majority are vegetarian.

All plants are our brothers and sisters. They talk to us and if we listen, we can hear them.
—ARAPAHO

The little-known religion of Jainism is also pacifistic and had its beginnings in India. Jains believe that animals and plants and human beings all contain living souls and are a perfect example of pure animism being practiced in a modern religion. Jains are vegetarians, but they also recognize the fact that eating plants does cause harm to them. They eat them only for survival and because they believe vegetarianism causes the least amount of violence toward living beings.

The Wicca religion is considered a pagan religion, but its adherents also worship and revere the Mother Goddess and prefer to live in harmony with all of nature. In that sense they respect all animal life as part of mother earth and have incorporated it into their religion. Many followers of Wicca were persecuted because the Church thought of them as not only pagans but practitioners of witchcraft, and many fell victim to the Holy Inquisition in its infamous purges. Interestingly enough, many pagan religious practices were incorporated into Christianity and are still followed today.

So you see most cultures and societies and even more ancient religions gave respect to and often worshipped animals. I believe we should give love and respect to what God has created for our enjoyment and care. If people would just realize that animals have feelings, maybe they wouldn't see them merely as a creation, but a creation with a soul, here to keep the earth in balance. Even the bee must pollinate or we won't have plants or flowers. Every creature has a purpose in God's huge plan, and to destroy even one species puts a hole in that plan of creation that has to be filled to maintain the balance in the order of things.

Today, dogs are certainly one of the most popular pets kept by humans, and they have been adapted for almost every type of life—from arctic sled dogs to jungle dogs to city dogs to those on a ranch or farm. Their instincts are fantastic, and there are many instances in which man trusts those instincts to not only help humankind in its work but also for protection. Dogs in the Arctic will take on a polar bear to defend their master, and know instinctively where there is thin ice and where they can find food. Inuits will be the first to say that without their dogs they might not have survived the bitter cold and environs of the North. After seventeen thousand years dogs seem able to interest us and understand our feelings and even our commands as no other animal can.

The British Isles and Australia and other countries with large herds of sheep would be at a loss without their sheepdogs. The complicated work these amazing animals perform is a sight to behold. I watched a farmer in Ireland with his Border collie for almost an hour as he directed his dog to herd his sheep from one pasture to another—it was fascinating and awe inspiring. With merely a few whistles and a few hand signals his dog knew exactly what to do, and the dog patiently and precisely maneuvered more than fifty sheep out of one pasture, down the road, and finally into another pasture. If you have ever watched a sheepdog you can see traces of the stalking procedure that wild wolves must have employed in going after game. They will move a few steps, lay flat and watch, get up and move some more, always driving the herd in the direction they want. They generally move slowly and purposefully, and will only break into a fast run and bark at or nip at sheep that try to break away, but they never hurt them in any way. I asked the farmer about his dog afterward, and he said this dog had been in his possession for only three years, and that she was young and not as experienced as his previous dog. "She sure seemed experienced to me!" I said, and the farmer just laughed and said that she was "coming along nicely."

Although many dogs are working dogs, the majority of dogs in the world today are pets. They give love, protection, and companionship, and there is almost a psychic bond that goes on wordlessly between pet and owner. There are more than four hundred different pure breeds of dogs, as well as thousands of mixed breeds, and humans are constantly making new breeds. I myself have a Labradoodle, which is a newer breed and is a cross between a Labrador and a poodle. I don't think this matters except for the fact that history shows how in the beginning dogs were used mainly for work and protection, and that over the years that aid and help to humankind has evolved to a point where dogs are more like our companions than our slaves. We still have wonderful working dogs and dogs to sniff out drugs and help the blind or the deaf, but now it's more common to find dogs that are loving companions—creatures that constantly give us joy and solace. They take up a place in our hearts and homes that nothing can replace. Even after Jolie died and I got another dog, a German shepherd that I loved dearly, there was and still is a place for Jolie, the same as every other dog I've had.

Animals are not only a part of our everyday life, but they have been assimilated into our modern culture in so many other ways. We have zoos to see them, nature programs and safaris to see them in the wild, farms to utilize their working abilities, ranches to breed them for food and clothing, research labs that experiment on them, hunters that hunt them, large ships to harvest fish or whales in huge numbers, not to mention our dear pets who are either loved or abused in any manner of ways. How we treat animals in general is a black mark on society, and we are finally getting some action by those involved in animal rights to help correct some of the abuses that just seem to go on and on. I have always felt that humankind will not only destroy this world we live in but will destroy the poor animals that also inhabit this planet and cannot defend themselves against our own lemminglike run of self-destruction. However, it's the way we treat the animals we love—whether by supporting animal rights as discussed in the last chapter, or by caring for the pets that have entered our own lives—that can ultimately save us.

3

OUR ANIMAL TOTEMS

"Every animal knows more than you do."
—**Nez Percé Indian proverb**

People who think animals are dumb and beneath us always seem to look at life with tunnel vision. They don't see the whole picture very well, and they certainly don't see how animals have and still do affect humankind. While doing my research I found that the diversity of thought about animals runs the gamut from those who think animals are dumb and should be used only to serve humankind to those who hold animals in the highest esteem and even worship them.

Humankind always seems to view and believe all things in extremes, which is good in one sense—it means that we can usually see all sides to a particular question and then various thoughts, theories, and philosophies develop from those viewpoints and beliefs. On the other hand, humankind knows very little in comparison to God, can be completely wrong many times, and has emotions that can create bigotry, hatred, war, and harm to the earth, animals, and other human beings because of the various extreme polarities of these viewpoints and beliefs.

I have found that people with true spirituality can usually understand all sides of a question, both good and bad. To understand something doesn't mean you have to embrace it or believe in it, but it is knowledge that turns into wisdom more times than not. A prime example of this is the whole concept of evil. The truly wise and spiritual person knows that evil exists as a form of "signpost" to help humankind define what is good, but then another problem develops because the definition of "good" is then taken to new polarities by humankind's own nature to view and believe in extremes. We also see this in the

various views of "evil" that you would think
would be easier to define and understand,
but it seems humankind cannot settle on
a universal belief that is either good or evil
or even what they mean by both. A sup-
posed sin to one person may be a cherished tradition for another. We see this
every day in the various cultural beliefs
and religions that populate this world.

Now you may ask, "What has this to do
with animals?" Just this—humankind will
always have various beliefs and customs
that will not change, and their various viewpoints and beliefs about animals will not
change either. Once you acknowledge
and accept the fact that humankind with
all its fallacies and beliefs is the only in-
habitant and creation on this planet who is
not perfect, you will find that your spirituality has raised a mark or two. If you realize
and accept that humankind is on this
planet to learn and is the *only* living organ-
ism on this planet with that distinction—
this again raises your spirituality several
points. And finally if you know and accept
the fact that this planet called Earth is only
a temporal school for humankind and not

the ultimate reality—this raises your spirituality another few points.

God gives us each a song.
—UTE

Anyone would be hard pressed to put
forth that animals are not perfect creations
by God; they are just different types of creations. Humankind has always compared
other creations with themselves, thinking
always that we are the highest of God's
creations. For this reason many humans
don't think that other living organisms have
souls, but how do we supposedly know
that? Do we presume to know God so well
that we can say that souls don't exist in
other living forms? Just because God supposedly gave us dominion over all living
things (according to the Book of Genesis
in the Bible), does that mean we can kill
and mistreat them? Could not the word
"dominion" also mean a *responsibility* to
care for and ensure the survival of all living things as many think it does? The im-
perfect makeup of humankind has made it
entirely irresponsible in killing off many

animal and plant species, raping the planet of its natural resources, and creating an environment of unnatural pollution that we will probably never recover from.

Animals on the other hand have done nothing to harm this planet. Those that kill only kill for survival or defense. Most contribute to the natural order of things in nature that helps to keep this planet habitable. Do you think that the different attributes of plants and animals are simply a matter of chance or by-products of evolution? There is a Divine Order in nature that keeps it stabilized and yet ever changing as the environment changes. Humankind is the only creation on the planet that has upset that balance and consistently continues to do so. Nature tries to compensate, but is not always successful and thus our planet is now in dire straits and we humans are directly responsible for it.

Animals give us so much and yet we continue as a species to hunt them, kill them, capture them, and abuse them. Just who is the most civilized? Could you as a human being do the following like certain animals can?

1. Could you survive in the wild for your whole life without tools or weapons?
2. Could you catch a fish with your hands?
3. Could you migrate without a compass or even know when it was time to migrate?
4. Could you carry ten times your body weight like an ant?
5. Could you know what you can and cannot eat in the wild?
6. Could you weave a bird's nest or spider's web?
7. Could you go through your whole life happy like an animal does?
8. Could you experience the moment like an animal does?
9. Could you get along with five to twenty other beings for your entire life and remain in the herd?
10. Could you spend hours resting and con- templating (perhaps in communion with God)?
11. Could you take hours a day to just be with your family and to simply play and hug and love like most mammals?

(The above is based on spiritualnetwork. net in the section on animal totems.)

The instincts and attributes of animals are so much better than those of a human being in so many ways, and we sometimes forget that fact. We certainly don't have the strength of many animals; we cannot fly like birds and insects; we cannot survive in harsh climates like many animals; we cannot navigate like most animals; we cannot swim like fish and whales and dolphins; we cannot get along with one another like most animals. In fact, all in all, human beings are kinda wimpy. It is only our brainpower and our invention of tools and weapons that have allowed us to survive. Some then say that our brainpower is why the human being is superior, but given a level playing field and only our physical attributes, human beings are not superior to many animals. Our brains may appear to be superior and may very well be, although we still cannot navigate like a whale or dolphin or bat with sonar, and we certainly don't have the highly tuned instincts or the heightened senses of many animals. The point is that we are different creations, and each creation has different attributes for its survival—and we as human beings should respect that fact. Animals aren't necessarily better or worse than we are, they are just different, and we should acknowledge that they have just as much right to survive as we do.

Listen, or your tongue will make you deaf.
—TRIBE UNKNOWN

ANIMAL TOTEMS

One of the aspects of my belief in God is that God sends help to all of His/Her Creations. Yes, I believe in both a Mother and Father God and I believe that duality is manifested in nature to show us that fact. Just as the little and small bee is a helper to so many plants in pollination, we can see the many animals and plants that help one another in nature such as the pilot fish cleaning the parasites off a shark's teeth and body. I have always said that God sends us help through our spirit guides (such as my spirit guide Francine), and guardian angels and I would have no reason not to believe logically that God also sends help to animals and plants as part of their creation. One of the aids that God sends human beings besides spirit guides and angels is animal totems. I have mentioned animal totems in some of my other books, but let's go into this subject at greater length.

Webster's dictionary defines "totem" as any entity that watches over or assists an individual or group of people, such as a family, clan, or tribe. "Totemism" is a religious belief associated with pagan and nature-based religions that has an animal or other naturalistic figure spiritually representing a group of related people such as a tribe or clan. Totems have been with us since the first beginnings of humankind. Many of the ancient tribes would have a totem such as a bear's head or a deer's head on a pole to signify their particular clan or tribe. These primitive totems evolved into standards and flags in the modern-day world. So you could say that the star-spangled banner is the totem of the United States of America.

Totems have much more significance than just as identification markers. In ancient times as well as our modern world the totem was and is a spiritual symbol of the individual or group; and represents who they are and the characteristics that they embrace and believe in as well as being a symbol of their intrinsic makeup. Most totems are symbolized by animals and can represent the traits of those animals as observed by human beings. Therefore, a clan or tribe that utilized the bear as its totem might have one or more of the many attributes assigned to bears such as: industriousness, instinctiveness, healing, power, sovereignty, guardian of the world, watchfulness, courage, willpower, introspection, self-preservation, or great strength.

Francine, my spirit guide, says that my animal totem is an elephant. Elephants have the following attributes: strength, power, affection, loyalty, royalty, and wisdom. The attributes of animal totems come from human observation of the animal and then interpreting its actions into strengths, weaknesses, and human emotions. Depending upon which part of the world a particular animal inhabits, its attributes were defined by the ancient human cultures that resided with it. Perhaps the culture best known for using animal totems is the Native American, and many Native American tribes in Alaska, Canada, and the Pacific Northwest made totem poles that acknowledged these animal totems. One of the main totem animals of the Native American Plains Indians was the buffalo because it fed and clothed them, but many tribes such as the Sioux encouraged and had rituals for individuals to find and interact with their own particular animal totem, whether it was a bear, eagle, hawk, beaver, or another species.

One of the many misconceptions of modern man is the belief that ancient man—such as the Wiccans, pantheists, Indian shamans, Aztecs, Incas, and others with their pagan religions—was not as spiritual as we are today. This is a complete misunderstanding, because in many ways their worship of nature and animals is a much more spiritual way of life than the lives that many of us live today. I have related in some of my other books about how much of paganism was "christianized" by the early Christian Church and incorporated into church rituals that we still practice today. Many pagan rituals and practices are beautiful and spiritual in every way, and only the ignorant would not call them so. The Native American use of totems was not only one of respect and worship but also one of identifying with a certain animal and taking on the characteristics of the animal, whether it was bravery, cunning, wisdom, and so on.

My spirit guide Francine says that every person in life has his or her own totem animal, which is like an extension of some of our personality or essence. Really it isn't much different from those who believe in astrology and who feel they take on some of the negative or positive of their birth sign, or numerologists who try to find some insight into what people are like through numbers. It seems humankind has always tried to find the meaning of who they are, whether it's through animals, astrology, numerology, consultation with seers or psychics, or any number of other ways.

Wisdom comes only when you stop looking for it and start living the life the Creator intended for you.
—HOPI

Our personal totem animals can align themselves with us from a past life or can be written into our Chart before we come in—much like our spirit guides and angels that are allotted to us to make our journey through this learning plane easier. They don't interfere with what we have written, but they silently protect us in ways that we may never be aware of. Many believers in animal totemism say that we have differ-ent animal totems for different phases of our lives. I personally believe we have one totem animal, but I also believe that our animals and pets that have passed over will follow us, visit us, and come around to protect us in dangerous situations. I have had two situations personally in which I know I was helped by animals, one by my totem animal and one in which Francine told me a past pet helped me.

The first instance was many years ago when I was investigating a haunted house. This was for a very renowned doctor in my area and out of desperation he called me to cleanse his house. It seems that he and his family would constantly see an evil-looking face peering in and manifesting itself in their bedroom windows. When I first went into the house I found it very de-pressing and knew an evil act had been done there. I found the spirits of an elderly couple that had lost their daughter, but they seemed to be just lost souls looking for their girl. In the master bedroom I found the real problem with the house and was able psychically to view what had happened there.

It seems that there were two brothers, one of which had a beautiful wife. The single brother fell in love with her and was also mad with jealousy. This brother one night in a fit of rage and jealousy killed both his brother and his brother's wife, stabbing them both innumerable times—it was a very bloody scene, and an extremely violent act done in rage by a person whose mind just snapped. The face in the windows was this mentally ill brother looking in on his brother and his brother's wife just before he killed them. Later, we decided to leave, but we left two tape recorders on to see what we could capture. Many investigators use equipment such as EMF (Electro Magnetic Field), Negative Ion, and EVF (Electronic Voice Phenomena) detectors, as well as IR (infrared) thermometers when doing an investigation. I've been on haunting investigations with that equipment go-

ing full blast, but have found most of them
to be overrated in detecting ghosts. IR
thermometers are good for detecting cold
spots, but I've found the most success
with just infrared film (backed up by a digi-
tal or normal film camera) and the good
old cassette recorder or reel-to-reel recorder for longer recording.

When we came back the next day, we
picked up the tape recorders and techni-
cians started listening to the recordings.
As long as I have been in this occupation,
seventy-two years a psychic and fifty-four
years as a practicing psychic, never a day
goes by without a surprise! I was called
that same day to come and listen to what
was picked up on the tape recorders.
There was a lot of whispering on both tapes
that we couldn't decipher, but the most astounding thing was the deep resonant
sound of a dog barking that came in as
clear as a bell. Having had many dogs I
could tell by the timbre of the sound that
this was a large dog, but what was even
more amazing was the fact that only one
of the recorders had recorded the barking!
If both recorders had picked up the very

distinctive and clear barking you might be able to say a neighbor's dog was barking (even though we checked and no neighbors had any large dogs) or that a barking dog passed by the house. The one tape that had the barking only had it at various intervals over the course of several hours of tape. I was so confused and I asked Francine what in God's name was a dog's barking doing on the recording. She said that in one life I had a mastiff and it came along with me on the haunting and then stayed there when I had left, and in its spirit form was barking at the earthbound spirits that were there. Not to be confusing, this is not my totem protective animal. My totem is an elephant as I mentioned before, but Francine said the mastiff took over as protector.

I was not, unfortunately, able to release the mentally deranged brother so that he could pass over. This is not unusual for very traumatic scenarios that create hauntings. It seems that the tremendous amount of negative energy involved can create what I call an "energy implant" (energy both positive and negative can be so powerful that it literally remains trapped in the atmosphere), but in most cases of violence there is derangement involved and many times you cannot reason with or get a deranged ghost to listen to anything you have to say. Needless to say, the brother who was haunting the house just became more agitated and hostile when I tried to get him to listen and go forward through the white light to the Other Side. The doctor eventually had to sell the house because it was just too much for his family to bear.

Everyone has a spirit animal that comes with them in any incarnation, but that still doesn't mean that pets we have had that are on the Other Side won't jump in when needed. Even though we incarnate with spirit guides, angels, totem animals, and, of course, protection from God, it seems we can never have enough. I'm sure that's why the Native Americans made the totems of the animals that they felt looked out for them.

I have a very dear celebrity friend who had parked her car in an underground parking garage. It was late when she got out of her meeting, and the parking lot was pretty empty. All of a sudden she was walking to her car and heard footsteps behind her. Her spirit totem animal allotted to her happened to be a cobra. As she turned she saw this man advancing on her with a ski mask on. She had nothing with her to protect herself. All of a sudden she got the idea to not only call on her angels but to also call on her totem animal to protect her. She said she really felt something come in front of her. She even felt that she got bigger and stronger and conjured up the image of the cobra standing on its tail with its great hood spread out in the position to strike.

If a man is as wise as a serpent, he can afford to be as harmless as a dove.
—CHEYENNE

The man, she said, stopped dead in his tracks and turned and ran. Wouldn't you give anything to know what he saw, but you can bet he saw something paranormal, because he was hell-bent on getting away from her. She was more than relieved and couldn't get home fast enough to tell me about what she knew was her totem that had saved her.

The last episode to show you how our totem works firsthand took place when I went to the Winchester Mystery House in San Jose, California. It is a strange mansion built by the wife of the man who invented the Winchester rifle and is one of the spookiest and convoluted places you'll ever experience. According to legend, Mrs. Sarah Winchester, upon becoming a widow, had tremendous guilt over all the people that had been killed because of her husband's invention and was even afraid that she would be haunted by their spirits. She consulted a medium in Boston who reputedly told her that her family was cursed by all the spirits that had been killed and that they would only be appeased if she moved west and built a house for herself and the spirits. The medium told her that she must continually build to appease the spirits, and that if she stopped building she would die. Thus, Sarah Winchester moved from New Haven to San Jose and bought a small farmhouse on approximately 160 acres. She then hired workers of every type and started building onto the farmhouse. The building never stopped for 38 years, and was carried on 24 hours a day for 365 days a year. The mansion in its heyday was up to seven stories tall, but the 1906 earthquake in San Francisco toppled the top three stories. Today it has about 160 rooms, 47 fireplaces going to 17 chimneys, 3 elevators, and several basements and outbuildings on about 4.5 acres of land. The Winchester House is a tourist attraction today because of the strangeness in its building—with stairways that lead to nowhere, cupboards that open onto walls or thin air, and stained glass windows of spiderweb design. The number 13 is a motif throughout the house, such as thirteen steps to every stairway. It is definitely the project of an eccentric mind, and the house is supposedly haunted (in spite of Mrs. Winchester's best efforts to the contrary!). Some of the staff who worked on the premises had seen strange things, which is why I was called to investigate. I had heard stories, but prefer not to be briefed on any knowledge or happening before an investigation because I want to go in fresh and not be influenced by known stories or so-called "urban legends."

It was after visiting hours when I arrived

at the house, and a crew was setting up cameras and equipment in the room that apparently was having the most haunting activity. While that was going on, my ex-husband and I were to wait in the court-yard. We had been told earlier that they had a very dangerous German shepherd guard dog that protected the property at night. I remember saying, "Yes, but you're not going to let her out until we get back inside." I was assured that in no way would they let "Princess" out.

So we went out and sat on a bench un-der a tree, and I was sitting there admiring the garden when I heard a door open and out comes this huge German shepherd I knew must be Princess. You could tell she was a guard dog because she began to sniff the ground and started to go to the edge of the garden. I knew it would be only a matter of seconds before she made her way over to us, because apparently she hadn't caught our scent yet and was still looking around at the ground. I was look-ing at where we were and where the door was and how close the dog was, and I knew we'd never make it to the door. It was at this time that Princess looked up and saw us and we both froze. I started to pray and all of a sudden Francine said, "Your elephant totem has shown up and Princess can see her." I call my totem "Tembo," the Swahili name for elephant. As soon as she said that, Princess began to prance and move away from us. She was jumping and playing. I could now see Tembo was swinging her trunk and playing with Princess. I knew she wasn't afraid because she probably had never even seen an elephant, but I'm convinced animals know animals and have their own language and posturing. Tembo kept leading her farther away and my ex and I ran like the wind to get inside safely. I had a few choice words for the manager and for whoever had let Princess out because her reputation was legend in keeping intruders out. They were full of apologies and said apparently the security guard had not been told we were out there. You see some people would have blamed the dog if anything bad happened, and yet this is unfair because Princess was doing what Princess was trained to do.

This just shows that at the beginning of

the care and worship of animals, primitive man knew more about animals than we do and through the annals of time we have lost the love and respect these beautiful creatures deserve. I have seen wild animals attack when they are threatened, such as in Kenya when the farmers are infringing on their territory and they have nothing to eat. As we grow in population we begin to encroach on their land and like the Native Americans or any group of people, animals are going to fight for their land and food and survival.

When a man moves away from nature his heart becomes hard.
—LAKOTA

It reminds me of the elephant that killed his trainer in Hawaii, but later we found out that the animal had been mistreated and tortured; or the tiger from the San Francisco Zoo that jumped the retaining fence because it was alleged that she had been taunted, and yet in the end the animal was killed. Sure, there are renegade animals just like people, but compared to the insanity that goes on with our murders and senseless killing and wars the so-called uncontrollable animal is not even on the scale compared to what humankind does to one another.

So you can have your dear pets from this life or other lives and your animal totem that comes into life with you and protects you. We have spirit guides, angels, and loved ones who have passed over that also protect us and help guide us. That's why we should never feel alone ever. Nothing, absolutely nothing, is lost that God creates and we have all existed with God since the beginning of time or like my guide says—always. They are here to be our loving helpers, companions, and protectors.

In the next chapter, we'll start to understand how the pets we love travel to the Other Side, and what life is like for them once they cross over. And in the chapters that follow, I'll share amazing tales of my own experiences with animals, as well as the experiences of dozens of other people—stories about the psychic abilities of animals, of the grief of animals and their owners when a pet passes on, of animal bravery and protection toward their human companions, and of the love and communication experienced between humans and animals.

4

ANIMALS ON THE OTHER SIDE

"All who have died are equal."
—**Comanche Indian proverb**

Many people over the years have asked me how I get my information about the Other Side or as some people prefer to call it "heaven." It's a fairly simple question to answer and the answer is basically always the same—from my spirit guide Francine. Over the many years we have been together, she has literally given me tomes of information on a variety of subjects, but the information she has given on the Other Side has been embraced by millions. Naturally since she *is* on the Other Side she has firsthand knowledge of the Other Side and all that it contains, thus becoming my resident "expert" on all that takes place there. The information she has given has been validated time and again by my research in near death experiences and in hypnosis regression.

I think it is appropriate at this time to give you some information about Francine for those of you who are not familiar with her. I have given information about her in almost all of my books because she is such a source of reliable information. Francine has been taped and transcribed and utilized in so much of my writings about the Other Side, history, religion, lost civilizations, and numerous other subjects. She has been with me all of my life (as any spirit guide is), but she first made contact with me when I was a little girl of seven.

That first contact was exciting to say the least! I was brushing my hair at the dresser in my room when all of a sudden I heard a high-pitched feminine voice. It came out of thin air and said, "I come from God and you have nothing to fear." Now, being seven and alone in my room, I did what any normal girl of seven would do—I ran screaming from the room in fright! I fled to the person I trusted more than any other—my grandmother. As I've said, my grandmother was a very well-known local psychic in Kansas City, Missouri, and after calming me down and allaying my fears she explained to me that the voice that I heard was from my spirit guide. She had told me all about spirit guides earlier and how they were different from guardian angels. She had even briefly told me that she had "voices" that talked to her. Even though I was only seven, I knew that grandma was special, but I never dreamed that I would hear a voice like she did. Grandma always said that she knew I was psychic, but she didn't know if I would hear my guide like she heard her guides. Now that it had happened, she smiled and gave me a great big hug and said, "See, now you're special, too!"

Grandma encouraged me to talk to Francine (whose real name is Iena). Whether I couldn't pronounce it right at my young age or didn't like the name Iena, I still don't know, but I promptly gave her the name of Francine and it has remained that way since. I do have several other guides, but Francine is my primary one and the only one I can hear. The ability to hear my guide is called *clairaudience*, and her voice I'm sure is very nice, but it has always had a high pitch to it that sounds like Alvin and the Chipmunks or an opera singer on a high note after inhaling helium. Needless to say, although I love her dearly, her voice can be irritating if she talks to me for a great length of time. She has explained to me that the pitch of her voice is a problem because she is communicating from a different dimension than mine that has a higher frequency, resulting in the high, squeaky sound of her voice. Whatever the reason, her voice can be tough to listen to and it gives me a headache at times!

As I grew to young adulthood, Francine said she could come into my body and communicate with others. This sounded a lot like possession to me, and having been raised as a Catholic I resisted that option. But she kept at me about it. To be honest, I was afraid to let her come into my body, because I had been programmed that once possessed, the spirit would never give me my body and mind back. Finally, Francine took matters into her own hands, and while I was in a hypnosis class she came into me and put me into a trance state. I've explained the particulars in other books so I won't go into it here, but Francine said she did it to show me that no harm would come to me and that is the only time she has ever come into my body as a trance medium without my permission.

I am what parapsychology defines as a *deep trance medium*. I go into a trance state in which a spirit will enter my body and then communicate using my vocal cords. I never have any memory of what transpires during these trance states, and although Francine, as my spirit guide, is the one who generally enters, I have had many other spirits enter, including one of my other guides named Raheim, who has entered into my body numerous times to give out information. Francine says that when I give permission she then controls who will enter my body and also how they enter, in order to create as little stress to my body as possible. She has always advised me who will be entering before I trance, and I have never had any problems in what must be the thousands of trances that I have done over the years.

My deep trance mediumship and clairaudience have always been what I consider to be a gift from God, and over the years I have grown comfortable with them. Francine never helps me with my readings, however, always telling me that if she helped me, then my own psychic ability would not be as good as it is. Interestingly enough, she only volunteers information about me and my life infrequently (I suppose because she knows I have to follow my Chart on my own), but she does often volunteer information on other topics that she thinks I might be interested in. Francine will always try to answer any questions I put forth to her, but again she can be somewhat vague when it comes to questions about my life and loved ones. When she gives me one of her short or vague answers on my own life, I know she knows more than what she is saying, but I also know she probably can't really give me all the information she knows because it might interfere with my Chart. (For those of you who do not know, a Chart is simply a plan that a person makes on the Other Side with their own free choice about the life that they will live on the Earth plane, so that their soul can learn and become more spiritual for God.)

Francine is truly a dear and loving companion who has helped me greatly in my work and writings, not to mention the countless numbers of people she has helped and counseled when I go into trance in certain salons or research group gatherings. People who have listened to her and her counsel say she is never wrong, and I have never had an instance reported in which she has harmed or lied to anyone. I've only had reports on how she has helped so many, and for this I am truly grateful to her. It's through Francine that I've learned a lot about life on the Other Side, including our relationship to animals and how we continue to interact with them, even after they've passed on.

**When you die, you will be spoken
of as those in the sky, like
the stars.**
—YUROK

Animals on the Other Side

When animals die they immediately go to the Other Side. The Other Side is a perfect environment sustained by God, so you won't find yourself swatting mosquitoes (and your animals won't be scratching at fleas!). As I have explained in my other books, the Other Side contains all of the beauty that the Earth plane does—and then some. The Other Side has none of the ugliness and certainly none of the negativity that the Earth plane contains. The passage of animals to the Other Side is basically instantaneous; their souls just pass through a brightly lit portal or gateway from our world to the next. This is true for our pets as well as the many wild animals that also go to the Other Side, where there are vast herds roaming about. The Other Side also contains animal species that have become extinct, such as dinosaurs, and many of us when we are on the Other Side will view and interact with them.

Unlike the Earth plane, on the Other Side there is no need to eat, and therefore there are no predators or prey. It is truly a place where the lamb lies down with the lion. All animals are docile and tame and playful. Herd animals and birds will flock together; fish will form schools, whales will form pods, and on and on it goes. Animals of the same species gather together for companionship and play. Many species will even interact with one another in play, and mischievous species such as monkeys can be seen riding on the backs of horses or even tigers (as Francine told me she saw one time).

Animals that die and pass over to the Other Side immediately have reunions with their friends in the animal kingdom that they knew before they came into life on the Earth plane, just as we humans do with our loved ones. Animals, as I've stated, don't reincarnate, and do not take different forms, and we humans don't come back as animals. God keeps the phyla pure. We humans are the only ones who have something to learn, whether that is patience, tolerance, how to combat negativity, or one or more of a myriad of lessons that we choose to go through.

Animals don't have to write out a Chart for their lives like we do to learn from God. They also don't have to review their lives like we do, and when they go back to the Other Side they just play and romp. One of the levels on the Other Side (or "heaven" as some prefer to call it) is the animal husbandry level, where some of us decide to spend eternity with animals, nature, and horticulture. Others of us go into some type of research or the arts, or into counseling to help people going into and coming back from life on the Earth plane. Animals never need counseling or to be "cocooned" (a form of sleep therapy) on the Other Side because of a traumatic life like some of us humans do.

My career on the Other Side is that of counseling for incoming and outgoing souls, but I spend an inordinate amount of time with the animals, and especially all the animals I've loved and cared for during my various incarnations. Francine said to me once that when I come back home to the Other Side, it's hard for my loved ones to get to me because all my animals congregate to welcome me home. That's great because while I have loved many people in my life, I have to tell you there are many animals I've loved a lot more than some people I've known or met! My animals have never been unfaithful, lied, stolen, defamed, or hurt me in any way. They are pure entities with no agenda except to be with us as friends and partners along this road of life. I can be in a funky mood, and yet when my

Shar-Pei or Shiatsu comes up and nuzzles me as if to say, "I'm here and everything will be alright," you can't help but smile and give your pet a good hug.

When animals pass there is no confusion on their part as there can be with human beings. As their soul leaves their earthly body, they immediately see a brilliant white light and go toward it and through it, to be met by an angel. The angel then takes them to any of their animal friends they want to see or to reunite with others of their species. In the case of pets the procedure is the same, except that they are taken to a passed over loved one or their owners on earth after uniting with their animal friends. For example, my father, who passed away some years ago, is on the Other Side taking care of several of my pets who died after he did. I have many friends and loved ones on the Other Side taking care of the many pets I've had who have passed in this life and other lives. Francine says I have so many pets and animals on the Other Side that it sometimes borders on the ridiculous, but I love them all dearly!

I'm convinced that the reason animals never become earthbound "ghosts" is because their souls are so pure. Human beings can become tainted by the negativity of the Earth plane, and a few can become earthbound or what we call "ghosts" due to trauma, mental illness, and so on. Although the number of ghosts is less than 0.1 percent and 99.9 percent of humans make it to the Other Side without any problem, 100 percent of animals make it to the Other Side. As I've explained in many of my books, human beings who are "dark entities" (those who have chosen to be in opposition to God) are never allowed on the Other Side because there is no negativity there. Interestingly, there are no animals in creation that are considered dark.

Here again we must just realize that animals and humans are different types of creations and have different types of souls. I'm convinced that animals were created to be a help to humankind and to be an integral part of the order of creation. Unlike humans or other creations with humanlike qualities that live on other planets, they don't have to learn anything in a negative environment such as the Earth plane. They exist as part of the environment and can be utilized to aid humankind, but they must also be taken care of and respected and nurtured like we ideally would want to do to our environment. To see animals, living things, and resources abused and destroyed is truly one of humankind's greatest follies, and future generations will have to deal with it.

As I have related in many of my books, when a human being passes over to the Other Side, their knowledge of creation and God opens up and their brain operates at full capacity (as opposed to 10 to 20 percent of capacity in life on the Earth plane). In the case of animals, it is the limitations of the human brain to operate at full capacity on the Earth plane that makes it appear that animals don't have the intelligence of humans. When human beings and animals interact on the Other Side, they have telepathic communication that is not unlike a normal conversation with another human. Yes, there are distinct differences because again animals and humans are different types of creations, but animals can and do communicate regularly with us when we are on the Other Side— they are definitely not dumb!

We can then see that animals on the

Earth plane are perceived as stupid and dumb by many, not because they don't have the intellect but because we humans in life cannot utilize our brains to communicate with them like we do on the Other Side. How's that for irony? Some of us have better communication with animals than others, but it still does not even come close to what kind of communication we have with animals on the Other Side.

To get some sort of idea about the intellectual capacity of animals, just consider the following. Most animals have greater sensory attributes such as hearing, seeing, smelling, and sensing than human beings. Some have talents that we as humans will never be able to accomplish on the Earth plane, such as sonar navigation and the directional abilities of certain species, diving to deep depths in oceans, or the stamina and strength to lift many times their own weight. What we don't realize is that animals have brain capacities and sensory inputs that far outweigh our own in many areas.

Like human beings, animals on the Other Side are also in paradise and like human beings don't have to eat or sleep. Interestingly, one of the main differences between animals and human beings on the Other Side is that humans choose avocations and vocations and have an outward and inner desire to keep on learning. Again, we must remember that animals and humans are different creations and each serves God in their own way.

Even a small mouse has anger.
—TRIBE UNKNOWN

In doing my research for this book, I came across a beautiful poem that is known by many animal lovers entitled *Rainbow Bridge*, which I think all will enjoy.

The Legend of Rainbow Bridge
by William N. Britton

**Just this side of heaven is a place
called Rainbow Bridge.
When a pet dies who has been
especially close to a person here
on earth, that pet goes to Rainbow
Bridge.
There are beautiful meadows and**

grassy hills there for all our special
friends so they can run and play
together.

There is always plenty of their favorite
food to eat, plenty of fresh spring
water for them to drink, and every
day is filled with sunshine so our
little friends are warm and
comfortable.

All the pets that had been ill or old are
now restored to health and youth.

Those that had been hurt or maimed
are now whole and strong again,
just as we remember them in our
dreams of days gone by.

The pets we loved are happy and
content except for one small thing.

Each one misses someone very
special who was left behind.

They all run and play together, but the
day comes when one of them
suddenly stops and looks off into
the distant hills.

It is as if they heard a whistle or were
given a signal of some kind.

Their eyes are bright and intent.

Their body begins to quiver.

All at once they break away from the

group, flying like a deer over the grass, their little legs carrying them faster and faster.

You have been spotted, and when you and your special friend finally meet, you hug and cling to them in joyous reunion, never to be parted again.

Happy kisses rain upon your face.

Your hands once again caress the beloved head.

You look once more into the trusting eyes of your pet so long gone from your life, but never gone from your heart.

Then with your beloved pet by your side, you will cross the Rainbow Bridge together.

Your Sacred Circle is now complete again.

From the book, The Legend of Rainbow Bridge, by William N. Britton. Reprinted with permission. legendofrainbowbridge.com

The poem above (to which others claim authorship for different versions) really catches the spirit of the Other Side and the symbolism is beautiful and captures the wonderful essence of friendship, love, and reunion.

One of the great benefits of the Other Side is that when you are there you can literally go anywhere you want, and that includes making visits to the Earth plane. Just as our loved ones who have passed over watch over us and visit us from time to time, so do our beloved pets.

I have received many stories from individuals about dead pets that came back to visit. For instance, Dorothy writes: "It was Mother's Day four years ago. I decided to do some ironing before my sons came to visit. After ironing for awhile I looked to my left and there was my dog Susie looking at me. Susie had been dead for fifteen years. She stayed with me for about fifteen minutes, and I spoke to her as I always did. I reached down to give her a pet and she was gone. Susie was the love of my life and there is never a day that I don't think of her. She made that Mother's Day the best one ever."

It was no accident that Susie showed up. She wanted that to be a Mother's Day present to her beloved owner, and also to show Dorothy that all life lives on and that she would be waiting for her. When the time or atmosphere is right we can tune into our beloved deceased pets, and this shows nothing is lost and that we will all be reunited in God's time in heaven or the Other Side.

There is no death, only a change of worlds.
—DUWAMISH

I can't even begin to tell you of the literally thousands of letters and e-mails that I have received about animals that have passed over to the Other Side, as well as countless tales about living animals that tap into their innate spiritual awareness to protect, warn, and nurture us. I've seen it in my own life—how before an earthquake my dogs run in a circle, or the time we had a prowler that they chased out of the yard. We should never take for granted what our pets add to our life. I feel the biggest thing they give us is their love, friendship, and companionship. When I'm down in the dumps or suffering from a bout of the flu, my animals often won't play as rambunctiously as usual; rather, they are more likely to sit silently beside me, like they are keeping watch and giving comfort.

But one of the most fascinating parts of our animals' behaviors is how they come back to visit us after they pass. If our passed-over relatives come back to visit and protect us, why should we be surprised to learn that the animals we have loved (and that loved us back) would return to show us they still survive and are waiting for us. This is no more evident than in the following story. Barb writes, "My brother had a Rottweiler named Della. She was an eighty-pound lapdog. My nephew Shaun adored this dog. Shaun died suddenly ten years ago, and their dog Della died four years ago. My granddaughter, who will turn four in September, told her mom that her friends Della and Shaun play with her at night and they make her laugh. She was afraid of her bedroom before, now she is not. We believe it is Shaun and Della with her!"

The best way to handle any situation with young children who see spirits—be they spirits of people, animals, or both—is to encourage them to talk about their experiences. The absolute worst thing to do is say it is just the child's imagination, or to downplay their experiences. Shaun and Della came to help with the fears of the granddaughter and to put her at ease.

If you are a pet lover like I am and adore your pets, you'll observe that they can sometimes stare down a hallway or even bark or hiss at what seems to us an empty corner. If you are really familiar with your dog you can also notice changes in his behavior. Some universities are even studying the difference in the barks of dogs. I can tell with my dogs whether it's a bark of warning, pain, joy, or playing, or even a bark saying *Will you please notice what I see . . .* This often happens when they see a ghost or a spirit. They never bark at my spirit guide Francine because she has been with me all my life, and I'm sure they just feel she's part of the family, but an unfamiliar spirit can set them off because it is a stranger to them. My Westie and Labradoodle are very protective and sometimes they bark when they become startled because they hear or sense something they cannot see. Troy, my Westie, has even been lovingly said to bark at falling leaves.

Francine said to me once, "Watch what I can do." There must have been six people in the room and my Shar-Pei and Westie were in the house. Francine went to the middle of the room and held her hand up like she was holding a treat. I could see it, but imagine the other people watching these dogs jumping and running right around her and being so excited. More than one asked, "What the hell is going on?" Often I'll be reading or writing and I'll see one of my dogs just get so excited and run in a circle and bark just like they do with us, and I know that Francine or another familiar spirit is playing with my dog.

Our loved ones from the Other Side can send us animals to comfort us. They don't become the animal or the bird; they just send the animal to give those of us who are living a signal from a living creature who can see and understand them. Why? Because they, the animals, are so close to God. Have you ever heard of an animal committing the crimes of human beings? I know that may sound ridiculous, but think about it. They just follow their own created aspect of being in the state of "Being."

Many times animals will send a messenger to tell us they're all right. One woman wrote that after she lost her dog she was in such pain. One day, a week after "Scruffy's" passing, she heard a scratching at the door. She opened the door and there stood a terrier just like the one she had just lost, although it was larger and had different coloring. After checking around the neighborhood and the lost-and-found ads, she adopted "Oscar" (the name she gave this second terrier). The amazing part is that she had a picture of Scruffy on the mantel and as soon as Oscar saw the picture of Scruffy he began to dance and bark like he recognized him. She said he kept this up for a week. She believes like I do that Scruffy sent Oscar to fill the void. It shows that animals not only make it to the Other Side or heaven but that they can communicate with one another there.

Speaking of this, I can't tell you the times my dogs will see a spirit in the room and just stare over in the corner or watch as they look above you. They are seeing your loved ones, your guides, or even your angels. I've always said that children and even

more so animals are the most psychic beings that exist, and I'm sure it's because not
only are they pure spirits but they have nothing to deter them. Their minds are not full of
all the "stuff" and worries we carry around.

People also come for animals when
they pass over as do other animals. No
one ever goes alone, and love like this
never dies. I've done so many readings in
which I'll see and describe passed loved
ones, and many times there is a beloved
pet with them that has also passed over
that I will also try to describe.

Colette writes: "When I was in my last
year of university, I spent a month in Scot-
land with my friend and his family. His parents had a dog named Bracken, who was
getting on in years and not doing too well.
The parents left for a couple of days for a
trip to Edinburgh, and on the second
night, my friend R woke up suddenly in
the middle of the night and said, 'Bracken
is dead.' We went out to Bracken's little
area and sure enough, he was gone. R
buried him under a tree because he didn't
want his mother to see her beloved pet
lifeless."

So what had made Colette's friend so sure that his beloved family dog was dead? As she would find out, it was because of an eerie link between this animal and a tragedy in her friend R's past.

"I guessed that R had dreamed about Bracken's death, because I've dreamed about things that have subsequently happened in waking time. When the time was right, I asked him if this was the case. 'Yes,' he said, 'I heard my son's voice saying, *Come on, Bracken*.' R's thirteen-year-old son had died a year earlier in an accident. It was the first time I realized that animals, too, have spirits. And I was overjoyed to know that my childhood Alsatian, my beloved Rex, was not lost to me forever."

This story demonstrates the linkage among all living things. Just as we humans never die alone—someone always comes for us to usher us to the Other Side—so too it is with animals. Sometimes animals are greeted by our loved ones who have already passed on, and, of course, sometimes animals come for one another. The next story also is an example of the telepathic communication that we have with animals on the Other Side, only in this case it took place in a dream.

Kris writes, "My Labrador, Zorak, died at the healthy age of nine years. My shepherd, Zilla, had died two years before him of cancer. Zorak had been sick for quite a while with kidney disease, and a terrible abscess three months before his death put him in the hospital for several days. He nearly died and was on IV fluids for four days. I was finally able to take Zorak home, and he slowly began to recover. Shortly after I brought him home, however, I had a dream that Zilla and Zorak were lying on the living room floor. I was so happy to see Zilla! He had his paw on Zorak's paw, and he communicated with me (he didn't actually speak, but I heard his words clearly). He said, 'I've come to take Zorak.' And I said, 'No, Zilla, don't take Zorak!' And he very calmly replied, 'He knows, he understands.' And at that moment I had a sense of peace and calm and I knew that Zilla would be there for him.

"Zorak finally lost his battle with kidney disease three months later. I was devastated, but I strongly believed that he was with his 'older brother' and was happy and no longer in pain. I still miss them both and dream of them occasionally."

With that same thought in your heart consider this—we have an all-loving, magnanimous God. Not a God of humanized, "baser" qualities such as vengeance, jealousy, greed, or anger—just all love. The other God is man-made. God is perfect and never flawed, and therefore God is all good. With that premise in mind, why would He or She ever destroy or neglect these marvelous creatures that He/She made to be loving companions and aids to humankind?

Everything the power does, it does in a circle.
—LAKOTA

Nothing that God has created is ever, ever lost. Everything on the Earth plane exists on the Other Side (heaven), except there is no cruelty to animal, vegetable, or mineral. We all find that the Other Side is basically the same topography as here, except it's in another dimension that is about three feet above our level. The Earth plane is the place of our learning for God, a school that unlike the Other Side contains negativity and all that it brings with it. When our time comes to pass over, we just go home and are reunited with all our loved ones and our pets and all the love and paradiselike atmosphere of the Other Side, which includes life of all kinds.

I've never really comprehended how we all fit over there, but my guide Francine says their laws of physics are different on the Other Side. Even though there are more animals and humans on the Other Side than on earth, the Other Side is not crowded at all—huge areas of open space exist that are wondrously beautiful. Francine says we all have a body that is in a real form, and that includes all animals. The wonderful thing about our bodies is the fact that we are all about thirty years of age on the Other Side, while animals are also young, playful, and frisky. Why thirty? Logic dictates that it is a perfect age, because it combines youth and maturity.

People who have had near death experiences, as well as thousands of people from every culture and religion who have had hypnosis regressions, report the same images of the Other Side. It's a remarkably consistent vision across all backgrounds and cultures! People also report seeing their pets and loved ones, all of whom appear young and healthy. However, when I "pick up" loved ones in my readings, they usually assume the last visage they had in life (or people wouldn't know them from my description!). The interesting part is that when I pick up pets they are almost uniformly young, healthy, and feisty.

In this next story about a visitation from a beloved pet who had passed over, the writer's description of the dog's colors is a validation of the brighter, more vivid colors that exist on the Other Side. It's a phenomenon that's been witnessed by thousands of people who have briefly seen the Other Side; they constantly bring up the fact that colors there are nearly indescribable, because we have nothing like them on our plane.

V. writes, "Several years ago, I was in an ICU unit battling pneumonia. Since I'm a kidney/pancreas transplant patient with a compromised immune system, the odds were not the best that I would survive. On one particular morning, I looked over at the side of my bed and saw my dog, Chelsey. Chelsey had 'crossed over' several years earlier, but at the time I was just overcome with joy to see her so I didn't dwell on how she had found me. I called her name and she moved up in the bed so I could pet her.

"On earth Chelsey was a brown dog, with the white trademark beagle stripe that ran down her nose and a white tip on her tail. However, now she had the most vibrant colors that I had ever seen. No colors on earth could come close to these colors—they were hues that only God could make. I continued to pet her and the next thing I remember, a nurse was asking me if I wanted something to drink. To this day, I believe Chelsey came to be with me in my hour of need. Needless to say, I can't wait to see her again!"

The Maasai and other tribes in Kenya believe that the elephants and other animals have souls. It's a concept that makes innate sense to me. After all, God isn't frivolous—He doesn't make mistakes, and He loves all Creation. Our Lord said even the hairs on our head are numbered. Now if love is that infinite, why let these precious souls fall into oblivion?

Even when we go to heaven (the Other Side) and into the Hall of Orientation (this is where we check in after we go through the tunnel after passing), our animals make it there first to greet us. What a blessed sight that must be. They are all young, healthy, and frisky and are full of energy and bursting with excitement to see us.

This next story gives us further details about the landscape and the essence of the Other Side—what it looks like, how our loved ones (especially our dear pets) can visit us and heal us, and the reasons they communicate so persistently with us. If St. Francis of Assisi could communicate with animals, others can, too. In the coming chapters, we will see how animals know more than we do, and have visions of what is to come far better than any of us.

Nancy writes about her horse Cheyenne, "I bought Cheyenne some years ago for my son. She was an unusually marked and beautiful paint Appaloosa, the type of horse that Native Americans would call a medicine hat Appaloosa. A friend had seen her at an auction and bought her just because she was in such a neglected shape. Cheyenne was grossly underweight, nothing but skin and bones. She was only five, and she was sweet natured and loved human attention. I would often tease her and tell her that she was my spirit horse.

"I had Cheyenne for about a year when one day she came home with a small hole in the thick upper muscles of her back leg. I assumed that it was a puncture wound, so I treated it and thought no more of it, but the next day it was worse so I called the vet. He also assumed that it was a puncture wound but the lesion continued to worsen.

"The second night she came to me through very intense thought (telepathy), and she let me know that she needed me to check on her. I, of course, freaked out, but I got out of bed and went to the barn and saw that Cheyenne was caught under a gate. We got her out from under the gate, but she was getting worse and none of our treatments were doing much good.

"The next morning I went to feed her and there she was standing in a large pool of blood. The vet arrived and found that she had broken her leg bone, which had hit a major artery. We couldn't save her and had to euthanize her. We think that someone was hunting and she took a bullet to the bone in her leg. It was a small caliber, but it weakened her bone and it caused the infection that we could not correct.

"Cheyenne later came to me again. She told me that she was in lush green pastures with tree-lined creeks and there were lots of birds there. She told me that she was fine and that she could come and go any time she wanted to do so. Later one of my cats got really ill. I kept taking her to the vet, but nothing was helping her. The vet wanted to put her through a lot of tests. Again my horse came and told me that my cat could not be saved and to not put a lot of money into tests and so on. The cat did pass away.

"There were other times later when Cheyenne would come to me. I would get a nervous energy feeling when she would come, but she would always tell me that it was her. Sometimes I would find out what had been going on at the time and sometimes I wouldn't, but I always knew it was her and that someone or one of my critters that I cared about was in trouble."

Nancy's horse Cheyenne was an amazing guide and a great comfort to her, no doubt in gratitude for Nancy's loving treatment of her during life. It's a reminder that the kindness and love we show our animals will grow and multiply, both in this life and on the Other Side.

This next story shows how animals not only meet one another when they pass but also go through the light just like we do. Gina writes, "I was so lucky to have a Siamese cat by the name of Lenny who chose me as his guardian and best friend. Lenny came into my life on a dark, rainy February 14 afternoon. He was my best friend—I always had someone warm to come home to, and I spoke to him as a human. He always knew when I was hurting, frightened, and in utter panic and he stayed as close to me as possible.

"My sister's cat was named Gigi. Lenny took Gigi as his own, protecting her and teaching her. One day Lenny even jumped into a tree three stories high (several times!) showing Gigi how to get down from a thirty-foot branch where she was stranded. I nearly fainted! He always protected her from harm.

"When Gigi died—years after Lenny had already passed—I had a beautiful dream. I saw a mist and a heavy gray iron arched gate, and there was my Lenny—beautiful, young, and whole. Opposite him was little Gigi, prancing down a smooth path and growing young, beautiful, and whole again. Lenny walked majestically as he always had in life to meet her. There was a beautiful small gate with a warm glowing light radiating from it. They stood there, rubbing their faces together and giving kisses. Lenny walked her to the gate radiating light. He stood to her left as she trustingly walked through the gate into the light. He gave me a look of profound love, tranquility, and understanding, as if to say, *Everything is as it should be now.* He slowly turned and walked through the gate into the light with the gate softly closing behind him.

"After that I never grieved or mourned for him again. I was not afraid to meet the day, my insecurity healed, and I knew all was right once more. Thank you, Lenny. . . ."

Notice also in Gina's story how her cat changes to being young, beautiful, and whole, just like my guide says we all do on the Other Side. Many theological works talk about us being young and in a glorified body in the afterlife, even the Book of Revelations states this. Just as humans become thirty again when we pass over, so too do pets arrive at the Other Side in their healthy state.

It's amazing how our dear pets know how to ease our pain and make us feel whole again, both in this life and in the next. This next story is rather long, but in reading it I reached for my Kleenex box more than once because of the inspiration it contained. Lori writes, "Just by chance (and this word will factor in the story) I went to your Web site today and found that you were asking about pet stories, and I had to write and tell you mine.

"In 2002 we had our blond Labrador retriever Chance put to sleep. He had bone cancer and was only six years old. Chance was my then significant other (now husband) Jack's best friend. When Jack and I first got together I have to admit I was a bit jealous

of Chance, because Jack just showered
him with attention. Jack adored Chance
and vice versa. But once I was firmly en-
trenched in their lives I became Chance's
"mommy" and we became a wonderful little
family—Jack, myself, Chance, and Darby,
my beagle. Sadly in June of 2002, shortly
after moving to our mountain home, I noticed Chance lagging behind on walks and
then limping. He was a trooper, but we
found a lump in his leg, and our vet confirmed it was cancer. Jack refused to give
up on Chance, but he quickly went down-
hill. We knew what we had to do—one
September day we took him to the vet, I
lay next to him, and we said good-bye.

"Jack was inconsolable. Nothing helped.
He went home and went to bed—he was
heartbroken. Thankfully, I had my faith that
Chance went home and would always be
with us and waiting for us, but Jack just
didn't know if he could believe this—he
hurt so much.

"I went about trying to locate a 'new'
friend for Jack but couldn't find a litter of
blond Labs anywhere. Finally locating
some, we went to see a litter and Jack

held a puppy but he just knew it wasn't the "one." Then we found a beautiful guy and he was the biggest male just like we asked for, but the breeder had promised him to someone else so he fell through, too. We went home heartbroken and decided that we would wait until spring.

The soul would have no rainbow if the eye had no tears.
—TRIBE UNKNOWN

"That afternoon, something told me to check around one more time. I went on the Internet and searched the surrounding newspapers; all of a sudden up pops an ad for Labrador retriever puppies. I called and the lady who answered said, "I didn't think they were putting that ad in until Friday" (it was Wednesday), but yes they had a litter of puppies. She confirmed that she had blond puppies, and I told her we were looking for the biggest male she had. I quickly told her our story, and she said, "Well, I think your dog Chance has sent you to us." I asked her why and she explained that it was her son's dog that had the puppies and her son's name was 'Chance,' and the mother of the puppies was 'Chantal' named after her son Chance. Well, let's just say I was blown away. I knew this wasn't only a sign; this was a huge message to Jack that Chance was still here looking out for him just like he always had.

"We went to see the puppies on Friday (ten puppies in all) and they all came running out at once, but this plump blond puppy came up to Jack's feet and plopped down on his sneakers and pulled at his laces. Jack scooped him up and the lady said, 'That is weird, that is the biggest blond male puppy we have.' We knew that we had the 'one.' We did not have to pick him out because Chance had picked him out for us. Needless to say he went home with us, and C.J. (Chance Jr.) is now Jack's boy just like Chance was."

"I am attaching a poem that I wrote; for about a week each morning I would wake up, and I had more and more of this poem in my head. Well, I think Chance sent it to me to write; in fact, I know he did. Thanks to Sylvia and reading her books for so

long, I have no doubt that Chance is home,
with us, and waiting for us to join him when
our time comes."

I'm Still Here

Your heart has been heavy since that
     day—
The day you thought I went away.
I haven't left you I never would—
You just can't see me, though I wish
     that you could.
It might ease the pain that you feel in
     your heart—
The pain that you've felt since you've
     believed us to part.
Try and think of it this way, it might
     help you see—
That I am right here with you and al-
     ways will be.

Remember the times we were out in
     the yard,
You could not always see me yet I
     hadn't gone far.

That's how it is now when you look for
     my face—

I'm still right beside you still filling my
  place.

I find it to be so very sad,
That seeing and believing seem to go
  hand in hand,
The love and the loyalty the warmth
  that I gave,
You felt them, did not see them, but
  you believed just the same.

I walk with you now like I walked with
  you then—
My pain is now gone and I lead once
  again.
My eyes always following you wher-
  ever you roam—
Making sure you're okay and you're
  never alone.

Our time was too short yet for me it
  goes on—
I won't ever leave you, I'll never be
  gone.
I live in your heart as you live in
  mine—
An enduring love that continues to
  shine.

The day will come and together we'll be,
And you'll say take me home boy, and
**   once again I will lead.**

Until that day comes don't think that
**   I've gone—**
I'm here right beside you, and my love
**   it lives on.**

There is nothing that takes place by chance
(no pun intended). Just like our loved ones
can help us from the Other Side, so can
our animals. When my beloved father was
dying he looked up at me and said, "Sylvia, I can help you more from the Other
Side than I can here." It's true because
when I get upset or need something of
course I pray to God, my angels, guide,
and my loved ones, but especially Daddy,
and it always comes about or things work
out alright.

If we just keep our minds open we will
realize nothing is a coincidence. It's all
meant to be in our Chart that we wrote to
learn for God by coming down to this hell
we call earth. But if it wasn't hard how
would we know what we are made of and
how would we really learn?

I also loved the poem Lori wrote because sometimes when we feel pain we should write it down or even keep a journal. It's a way to release that pain, and a way to remind yourself with all certainty that you will see all your pets and other beautiful animals again on the Other Side.

God doesn't make mistakes. Sure, there are some awful people who *seem* like mistakes, but that's their own free will to separate from God. At the end of times, God just absorbs these dark souls back into the uncreated mass, like clay ready to be molded again. Meanwhile we and our loved ones and pets enjoy eternity, loving and enjoying one another.

This next story again shows us that not only humans but animals survive after death, and that many people see or hear their pets long after they have passed.

Miya writes, "I once had a one-year-old dog named Mohawk. Mohawk was a Pomeranian/spitz mix, and I loved him very much. I was eleven when Mohawk died. He liked to run and play in my grandmother's driveway, but one day she accidentally backed over him and killed him. We were both devastated, so my grandmother and I buried Mohawk in an old Creole cemetery in the woods near our home. After his death he would come and follow me to the bus stop, then wait for me to get on, and then he would disappear. When I got home he would again follow me to the house and then leave again. He did this for three weeks. After that I never saw him again. I'll always believe he wanted to make sure I was going to be okay."

This next story shows the spirituality of animals and how I've always believed they have their own angels. They don't need guides or Charts because as I've said they have one purpose—to love humankind, and even try to show us how to love and be loyal. If we could just absorb some of these attributes there would be no wars,

no greed, and no hatred. Some who have never had animals still can appreciate the love they feel for us and we for them. It reminds me of the way I felt about my students when I was a schoolteacher; I felt this love and motherly instinct for the children I taught, some of whom I'm still close to today. We don't have to give birth to someone to love them. I loved my foster daughter with all my heart. And I don't trust people who are cruel to animals and take a delight in hurting them. This is either a mental illness or an evil attribute that we should steer clear of.

Sara writes: "My pet Sean was gravely ill. I had to put him down. The doctor gave me a few minutes alone with him before she injected the lethal shot. Needless to say, I held him close to my chest as I recited Psalm 21 into his ear. I whispered into his ear how much I adored him and loved him. I said to him, 'Thank you for teaching me how to love.' In my heart I believed I would see him again.

"When I got back home without Sean, my other little pet Stephanie (a toy Pomeranian) looked up at me and for the *very first time ever* I heard her speak to me! I heard

Stephanie ask me, 'Where is Sean?' Her lips/mouth did not move, nor were there any other types of gestures, but I heard her speaking! I answered her verbally, 'Sean is in heaven with the angels now.' My little Stephanie just stared at me and then walked away. She behaved sadly for awhile.

"Later that evening I had a vision. I saw Sean resurrecting from his grave. He shook off the dirt from himself and started running toward a bright opening in the heavens, where there stood an angel with her arms wide open! About midway Sean stopped, turned around, and looked back at me! I smiled at him and said to him, 'That's alright baby, go on!' He took off running toward the angel once more.

"Then I heard the angel's voice say (as she bent down to pick up Sean into her arms) 'Hi!' The angel greeted Sean! Sean with his wagging tail leaped into the angel's arms and off they went."

Animals are the big reason why there is a level devoted to animal husbandry on the Other Side. If you have read any of my books on the Other Side, you'll know that there are six levels, each of which is devoted to a different vocation or pursuit—artistic, research and science, lecturing and teaching, orientation and record keeping, animal husbandry, and spirit guides. Of course, we can visit any level or area while on the Other Side, and my guide Francine says I spend a lot of time in the area devoted to animals. I think that to have a level devoted to animals also shows how much importance God puts on them.

Not only do our deceased pets meet us when we pass over but they stay with us on the Other Side, living in harmony with not only all our other animals but with all the beautiful animals God has created. I know we can't understand it right now (even though I've tried to explain it somewhat in some of my other books), but I'm sure we will. There is no time on the Other Side, but there isn't any large industry or large structured cities or pollution and high rises either. We will all know someday when we pass over, because from all the research I've gleaned over fifty-four years the Other Side does exist and, in fact, is the true reality of existence. Thousands of research subjects from every country, every religion, every color, and every walk of life report the same things without any reciprocation or contact with one another.

One of the things that just happened to me this last week again gives validation to this fact. A woman called the office and was holding her dying husband, and before he died he looked up at her and said, "Mary, I see it and everything Sylvia told us is true!" I was pleased and humbled, because I know it all comes from God— we who are blessed with the psychic gift are just vessels that information comes through. As we believe more in the truth of the Other Side, the veil between this side and the Other Side thins because belief brings out the truth and blocks negativity.

Now that you have a sense of what our animals experience as they travel to the Other Side, I'm going to spend the next chapter focusing on the sentient and psychic abilities of our animals—both those on this plane and those on the Other Side.

5

THE PSYCHIC ABILITIES
OF ANIMALS

"When we show our respect for other
living things, they respond with
respect for us."
—**Arapaho Indian proverb**

Whenever possible, I love to include true
stories in my books from people like you—
stories of actual psychic events that real
people have experienced. This book on
animals gave me a perfect opportunity to
gather these sorts of personal stories
about animals, a hugely popular topic and
one on which I have received so many
amazing tales. I put out a call on my Web
site asking for such stories, and I received
thousands of heartwarming and astounding notes from readers and fans. In addition, I heard amazing stories from the

thousands of people I've consulted with personally over my decades as a psychic, and the many thousands more I've met during my cross-country tours and live events. The material I received could fill fifty books.

In putting out a call for animal stories, I had no idea what kind of stories I would receive—the topic is so broad, and the issue is so personal. What I found to be amazing in receiving hundreds upon hundreds of animal stories was how many stories involved the sentient and psychic abilities that are so prevalent in animals, especially our pets. Maybe we can see animals in a different way after these stories that I'm going to tell you—that they are telepathic and sentient and know things psychically before we do.

I have always believed that an individual's makeup is a combination of life's experiences, cell memory (which includes experiences from other lives), and the spirituality that one has obtained and retained. We all have a spark of our divine God within us and we all experience for God. We can all learn from not only our own experiences but also the experiences of others. The hard part is to listen, observe, be aware, and then to retain these experiences for our own spiritual awareness and knowledge so that we can be the best possible person we can be. One of the hardest things for any human beings to do is to recognize themselves for who they are and to acknowledge their shortcomings. To do this you first have to see your own soul and the magnificence that God put there. All souls are magnificent and brilliant, but most don't ever realize that fact until they try to bring their soul to true spirituality.

Society and religion many times try to put a damper on human experience, especially those of a paranormal nature. Notice how in several of the stories in this book, the writer might refer to himself or herself as being thought of as "crazy." This is nothing more than a by-product of the programming we get from society or religion that tells us such experiences are imaginary, delusional, and never really happened. Being a psychic, I have critics and skeptics that throw barbs like this at me all the time. I know what I have experienced, just like all the writers of these stories know what they have experienced, and it isn't a question of delusion or imagination; the events they describe actually happened.

If we wonder often, the gift of knowledge will come.
—ARAPAHO

Animals Know When We Need Them

Anna writes that she was just sick about losing a bracelet that she cherished and which meant a lot to her. She finally and reluctantly gave up looking for it, but it haunted her because of its sentimental value. One day she let her dog Barry out in a part of the yard she rarely put him in, and he went straight to this one particular area of her lawn and scratched and then barked and looked up at her. He kept this up until she came over, and lo and behold there was the bracelet she had lost such a long time before which she had obsessed over.

Now consider that Barry had to know this caused her pain and knew what it was that she had lost—and not only that, but he found it for her. She said she kept hugging him all day and even played with him more out of gratitude. Think about how amazing it is that Barry knew she had lost the bracelet, or that he would even care. This shows telepathy, and even an image imprinted in his brain of what was making her unhappy. Now, we could say that a passed over loved one or Anna's guide communicated this knowledge to Barry and maybe that led him to discover its location, but this would still be an amazing feat because Barry did find the bracelet and knew enough to communicate that to Anna.

But sometimes the psychic abilities of the animals we love go even further, actually saving us from our own darkest demons. This next story shows that not only do animals sense our thoughts but also that we can learn to read their thoughts. In this case a simple look stopped an act that was wrong and senseless. Rachel writes, "At first when I read that you wanted people to send their animal stories, I thought to myself, *Well then, that's not for me. I've never been saved by a whale while drowning, or stopped from being killed by Lassie.* However, right when I was closing the Web site my dog came up to me and looked at me. Then I remembered a few years ago when I was having a really tough time. I was depressed and tired of living life. I decided to commit suicide one afternoon and actually had the pills in my hand when I looked down and saw my dog staring up at me. Just staring. I put the pills down and haven't attempted suicide since then. I heard dogs are good for lowering blood pressure and anxiety, but I feel that my dog truly prevented me from ending my life. The kind of look she gave me said, 'Why do you want to go? Who will I play with? Don't leave me yet!' This is how an animal saved my life. It may be small and no spectacular event, but I am still alive because of that look."

I for one *do* think it was a spectacular event. Every life is important, and I don't think any of us realize how we can impact the lives of others and how much help we can be to others just by living. Frank Capra's movie *It's A Wonderful Life* shows how Jimmy Stewart's character affected the lives of so many, and also shows how without the help of an angel things would have been different (and so much worse).

In Rachel's case, her dog knew she was contemplating suicide and got through to her with a look and some subtle telepathy that convinced her not to do it. Rachel still has a lot of life to live, and I'm sure she will help many in living it.

While some pets use their psychic abilities to save their owners from making big mistakes, other pets are seeking to communicate with us, but it's only afterward that we truly understand their meaning. This next story from Maureen not only explains why her cat acted in a particular way but again how sentient all animals can be. Maureen writes, "After a year of hospital ICU, I was able to bring my husband home on a ventilator. I nursed him alone five days a week, and on weekends my daughter would come and help me. He was home for six months before he died (with a few trips to the ER and one hospital stay during this time). Five days before he died, one of our cats, Samantha, who was a little standoffish, started to sleep all day on his hospital bed in our family room. When I would start to do all the caregiving I had to do, she would get up and meow and come between me and some of the

equipment. I had to do some pretty serious nursing on my husband—suction his
lungs, clean his trach, hook up his nebu-
lizer to the vent, clean his iliostomy, and
bathe him. There were times I would have
to 'bag' him because he felt he could not
get enough air (he was very sick). These
five days, Samantha would get up in my
face, almost in the middle of what I was
trying to do to help him. She left his bed
only to eat, drink, and use the litter box.
It is only in hindsight that I really think
she was trying to tell me he was dying,
because looking back I can see how he
deteriorated during that week, each day
getting weaker and weaker. Was she trying to help? Was she telling me to notice?
Was she telling me there was something
I should do? I think she was trying to help.
I know it pleased my husband that she
was close, but we did not understand her
actions."

The cat strangely was not only trying to
help but also urging Maureen to let her
husband go. It's not that Maureen didn't do
everything for her husband, but Samantha
was saying *He is going and he'll be alright*.
Animals have a real knowledge and under-

standing of not only this world but also of the Other Side, and lying close to him when he was ill was Samantha's way of giving her beloved owner a measure of comfort in his journey to the next world. If your pet has a sudden change in behavior (in this case, Samantha started sleeping on Maureen's husband's bed all day), it is usually for a reason. Animals will get especially close if a person is seriously ill or dying.

When I had minor surgery some years back, my dogs never left my side—they only left to go out and relieve themselves or to eat or drink. This had never happened before (and it's never happened since), but I haven't been as sick again as I was then.

Animals Sense Danger

These next stories also show the psychic ability of animals to save their loved ones. Autumn writes, "I have two dogs, a four-year-old yellow Lab named Wilson and a two-year-old retriever-chow mix named Max. Two years ago, we were having a very violent thunderstorm. There were tornado warnings in our area. Wilson had been pacing and whining in the living room. I was walking from side to side in our home, going from the living room to the kitchen to look outside. As I walked into the kitchen, Wilson suddenly jumped in front of me and tried to stop me from passing him. Then he started growling. Well, that just made me mad, so I started to push him out of my way, and he nipped at me! He had never done that. Just then, lightning struck our house. It struck exactly where I would have been standing, had I not been stopped!

"We smelled a strong odor of smoke and called 911. As it turned out, it was raining so hard, that it put out the fire on the roof where the lightning had first hit. All of us were safe that night due to Wilson."

If Wilson hadn't warned Autumn, the consequences could have been deadly. Wilson psychically picked up that a lightning strike was imminent, and also knew the exact location where it would come down! This dog must love Autumn very much; he even nipped at her and in doing so risked anger and punishment, all to keep her safe.

Francine says there is a "warning bell" that goes off in an animal's limbic brain.

Scientists don't seem to know what this part of the brain really does. The term "limbic" comes from Latin *limbus*, meaning "border" or "edge," and the limbic brain sits on the right side of our head just above our ear. This region is also called the "old brain" because it controls many of our basic instincts, such as emotion and behavior. Francine also says humans can also receive messages via our limbic brains, but because animals are so pure and simplistic their limbic brain is more pronounced. I personally feel that the limbic brain is where we can get direct communication with God.

Animals also are psychic and spiritual barometers. If a dog or cat has a generally loving disposition toward everyone except for one certain person, please be watchful and wary of that individual. Trust me, your animal is feeling something you can't sense or see. They are feeling the negativity that maybe you are blind to, and it's better to be safe than sorry. Nothing can warn you of negativity more than an animal can, and, in fact, animals can sense evil, more often than not, *better* than a human can. In this next story we see an example of this.

Shelley writes, "Around 1990 I was a full-time dairy farmer while my husband worked a forty-plus-hour job. My partner and fellow worker was my beloved dog Pepper. She was half Border collie and half wire-mouth heeler; both breeds make very good stock dogs. Pepper was my constant companion from the time she was weaned. We were inseparable, and on more than one occasion she not only helped me but probably saved my life. We had Jersey cows, a lovable and gorgeous breed of cattle, but the bulls are very mean. She guarded me and got me out of many tight jams with the cranky cows and bulls. However, that was not her greatest rescue.

"I have always been aware that animals and young children see way beyond this world and into the spiritual. Pepper was an animal who not only saw the spiritual but was able to relate this information to me through her eyes, thoughts, and gestures. The most astonishing occasion happened one sunny day when Pepper and I were alone at the farm. We had a regular 'soap truck' that worked for our milk company, and this truck would come by once a month to stock our supplies that we wished to purchase, such as soap, cheese, and so on. We had had the same driver for several years, so I was surprised one sunny day to see a new driver pull into our driveway. Instead of the usual truck, he drove a van with a trailer on the back. However, the sign on the side of the van did carry the milk company logo, name, and address.

"I was outside, as usual, and approached the van to talk with the man and let him know we didn't need anything right now. But when the man got out of the van, Pepper bristled like I had never seen her do before. Pepper was a loving, gentle dog and probably wouldn't bite anyone, so when she started snarling and growling at this man, it startled me. I stopped dead in my tracks, and she proceeded to get between me and the stranger. He asked if she would bite, and because of her reaction I said yes. He stood there with a flyer in his hand and told me the company had changed the route trucks to vans and trailers for cost savings. He opened the side of the trailer and asked if I would like to take a look at the contents. I told him no—it would be fine to just leave the literature and we would leave a list in the barn as we had in the past. At that moment Pepper looked me straight in the eye and I knew she was seeing something very evil. It was as if I could read her thoughts and she was saying, *Be afraid of this man and don't let him near you.* The man started toward me again, and when he did she turned toward him and barked in a vicious way that again startled me. I told the man that I thought it was best if he got back in his van, and I walked toward the house. He did get in his van, and Pepper stayed very close to my side until he pulled out of our driveway.

"When he left I sat on the porch with her and she laid her head on my lap, as she sometimes did, and she was literally shaking. She knew and saw something that I did not. My spiritual instincts are very keen but not nearly as keen as my faithful companion and pet.

"This whole incident puzzled me, so the following day I called a friend of mine, who was also with the same milk company and had the same 'soap truck.' Not only were they shocked but they also revealed that our usual 'soap truck' was just at their farm that morning—there was no new route, no new driver, and no new truck. I have no idea who the man was or what would have happened if Pepper hadn't protected me, but I will never doubt she saw the spiritual side of this man and it was not a pretty sight. I never saw this man again nor did anyone else on our milk route. God has protected me more times than I can ever count, and this time it was by my precious Pepper."

Pepper sensed something very evil about this man; he didn't belong on the route and she knew it. Whoever he was, he would have done Shelley real harm, and Pepper protected her.

I know firsthand the strong protective instincts that animals possess. When I was married to my first husband, who was a very abusive man, we had a German shepherd named Lance. If my husband even came near me, Lance would arch his back and bare his teeth; he never ever did this with anyone else. I noticed that whenever my husband was ready to go into one of his rampages, he would put Lance in the backyard. But Lance could almost sense that something was terribly wrong, and he would bark and literally throw himself against the door. I finally left my husband, and I realized that Lance knew the truth about him much earlier than I did. And we have the audacity to think animals are dumb?

Animals are a lot more intelligent and observant than we give them credit for. This next story shows the psychic or even practical knowledge of a pet that was protecting his owner from a wandering husband and his lover. She writes, "This story is about my beloved Midnight, he was a black cat (obviously). He was my baby and he passed six years ago last month.

"Midnight was a very loving cat. Everyone liked him—he was real sweet, very playful, just a real gem! I was married when I first got him. Some neighbors of mine became very close to us; they were a newly married couple. This couple was at our house a lot, but not always together. When I was working and my husband was home, she would stop by to 'visit.' She and my husband both worked odd hours, so I did not really think much of the time they spent together. She did laundry at my house, and they would sometimes go to the pool together.

"One night, as I arrived home from work,

Midnight followed me into the house and viciously attacked my neighbor's leg— clawed her up terribly, bit her, ripped her panty hose, and actually tore the skin with his teeth and made her bleed. He had never, ever done such a thing to anyone. We could not believe it! It was a few weeks later that I found out that this neighbor and my now ex-husband were messing around in my house!

"My cat knew it and was defending me; I know he was. I have always paid very close attention to all of my animals since then. Midnight was truly *my* cat, and he went with me when I left (obviously!). That was his way of telling me what was going on, and that he did not like it! Trust me, I always paid close attention to him around people when they came to my house after that."

So we can see that animals really do have a sixth sense about who is hurting their owner. Midnight realized that this other female was taking the place of his owner, and he wanted to defend her. If this isn't sentient reasoning I don't know what is. There is no other way to understand it except to realize that their intelligence and knowledge are much greater than most believe.

There is nothing as eloquent as a rattlesnake's tail.
—NAVAJO

Animals Are Intuitive

The Nez Percé say: "Every animal knows more than you do," and I agree. The more we study them, the more we will realize what cognitive abilities they have. The Sioux say: "With all things and in all things, we are relatives" and, of course, that means animals, too.

Animals are all heart and feeling and sensing. There are people who don't know some of the different problems humankind encounters as much as an animal does and yet we feel we are smart. Dogs and cats also have a telepathic sense, as this next story relates. Diane writes, "One Christmas Eve, my husband brought home a puppy. The kids were so excited, I could hear them squealing with joy all through the house. I looked at the puppy and said, 'That is the ugliest dog I've ever seen. Take it back from wherever you got it. I don't need one more thing to take care of.' Our children begged me to keep it. They promised me they would take care of it. All mothers know the truth in that statement.

"In the following months, that little wet black nose, big brown eyes, wiggly stump of a puppy grew into the most beautiful dog I'd ever seen. But she looked the same as she did when she was a puppy, so it must have been me who changed! I came to love her very much. She and I became soul companions. I swear she could read my mind. Whenever I came home and saw that she was sitting in the corner, I knew she had chewed something up. She was so smart! I couldn't punish her for it because she was already in the corner! What more could I do?

"Early one morning, before school, the kids and I loaded Aussie up in the car to drop her off at the vet for her annual shots. The clinic wasn't open yet. I decided to drop her off at my grandmother's house nearby and put Aussie in her fenced-in backyard. The plan was that I would call my grandmother from work and tell her about Aussie, then I would pick Aussie up after school and take her to the vet on our way home.

"I was a schoolteacher, and all heck broke loose at school when I arrived. In the craziness of the school day, I completely forgot to call my grandmother. After school, I picked up my kids and went to my grand- mother's house. What a shock when I got there. Since I hadn't called and my grand- mother didn't recognize the dog, she let it out of her yard. My Aussie had been run- ning around loose all day in a strange town. My grandmother was very sorry, but I knew it was my fault for not making the call. The kids climbed into the car and we went to look for her. We walked up and down every street in her neighborhood. My son Jason would start at one end of the alley between the houses and walk the alley and I would drive around the block and pick him up at the other end. The hours went by and the sun started to set. I told the kids that I didn't know if we were going to find her this evening—maybe we should resume the search the next day after school. Jason and Jessica started to cry. We looked some more. The sun set.

"I pulled the car over to the curb. Tears

came to my eyes. The kids were crying and saying they didn't want to go home without Aussie. I closed my eyes. With deep desperation in my voice, I demanded, 'Where is she, God?'

"All of a sudden, with my eyes closed, I saw a vision of Aussie in the Masonic Lodge Temple parking lot looking around for me. I told the kids, 'I think I know where Aussie is. Get in the car!' I drove straight to the Masonic Temple and there she was! Just as I saw her in my vision! She was so excited to see us I thought she was going to jump through the window.

"I couldn't believe it. What had just happened? What was that? I didn't know, but I didn't care. I had my Aussie back! Wet nose kisses and hugs everywhere."

I'm sure the dog was sending out signals to her family to be found, and Diane was in enough of a raw emotional state that she received it. Emotion can be a funny thing at times. In some cases it can help with psychic ability, and at other times it can block it. I'm convinced that the motive behind the emotion is the key, and that if your motive is pure, emotion becomes an aid to any psychic ability.

The behavior and actions of animals are incredibly intuitive. If people just paid more attention to their pets, we would see it's not just when we get out the leash that they know they are going for a walk, or when you get your car keys they know they may be going for a ride. Often they sense our behavior even without those visual cues, which I think is pretty amazing. Some may say this is just trained behavior or conditioned response, but isn't that how we all learn—by repetition and learned behavior? Watch any child and see if they don't know when they are going to eat, take a bath, and so on. So how is that different from an animal? And, in fact, our pets can know some things better than we do, for they sense danger, know grief, sense evil, and understand you better than humans can ever hope to comprehend.

My guide Francine says an animal will smell you not only to recognize you by scent but to sense your vibrational level and even (if you can believe it) to sense whether you are good or bad in intentions. This really takes them to a whole new level of awareness. As I said, we learn by listening or by mimicking behavior, and so do our pets. Listen to a dog in your neighborhood bark and soon all of the dogs in that neighborhood bark. It's almost as if they are saying, "I'm here, too, and I hear you."

Some animals don't like other animals, but this is also a human trait. Of course, humans don't growl (not usually, anyway), but I've met people I *would* growl at if I were an animal! Usually, animals will get along with one another unless otherwise provoked. Of course, we've all known or heard about a renegade dog that, because of abusive treatment or overbreeding, can suddenly "snap," but the truth is, don't we also have people like this? I'm wary of some breeds like the pit bull, because we hear stories all the time of pit bulls mauling and even sometimes killing people. Is it the dog's fault? I think the blame falls on the owners, who bred these dogs to fight and be aggressive, and brought out these unpleasant traits in their dogs as an extension of their ego, or to have the toughest dog on the block.

As intuitive as they are about us, animals are also intuitive about themselves and their own needs. My Shar-Pei Balooga for some unknown reason kept licking my ears. This had never happened before, and it was becoming aggravating. I knew there was nothing wrong with *my* ears, and then all of a sudden I realized he was trying to show me something about *himself*. I took Balooga to the vet, and sure enough he had ear infections in both ears. He was trying to show me his ailment by imitating or telepathically showing me what was wrong with him—*Look, my ears hurt so I'll show you by imitating where I am feeling pain*. I felt very stupid, and now I pay attention.

Animals are also very humorous and I can watch mine for hours. For instance, when my Labradoodle is getting ready to be fed she stands in the yard and jumps up and down like a pogo stick and does a type of pirouette a few times like a ballerina. It just puts me on the floor. Who doesn't laugh and get great enjoyment from watching a kitten or puppy? Their antics can be priceless, whether it is a kitten exploring a paper bag or a rambunctious puppy getting its cumbersome feet tangled up and falling down. Even today, one of the mainstays of the TV program *America's Funniest Videos* is the humorous actions of animals.

The actions of my golden retriever Kristen were more of what we might call subtle humor. Kristen was a large beautiful blonde dog who was caring and full of love and slightly overweight. Seeing that she might be somewhat lonely I began to collect other dogs as puppies. The first was a West Highland terrier, and Kristen, being fairly young, adopted Troy as her own. Some time later I got my Shiatsu and I noticed that Kristen, even though kind and nurturing, seemed to be a little put off with me. It was as if I could read her thoughts such as "What are you doing to me, having me be a mother figure to these dogs?" Then I acquired Misty the Lhasa Apso and for two weeks Kristen wouldn't even look at me. It was really a little disconcerting, but funny.

One day I went out and sat with her and put her face in my hands and looked into her eyes and said, "Kristen, I didn't get you to be a nursemaid to these dogs. Just let them play instead of you being the matriarch." I then got my Labradoodle and a Shar-Pei and she changed completely. Instead of being the central figure she would romp and play. No one can tell me they don't understand. They would pair up, with the large dogs playing together and the small dogs playing together. The only time Kristen got in the middle was when the little ones would fight over a toy. She'd come over like a mother and take it away from both of them as if to say—"If you can't share neither one of you can play with it."

I have been able to train my dogs not to relieve themselves in the house, not to chew, not to jump on people, not to destroy or dig, and so on. You may think this sounds very "woo-woo," but when I get a puppy I take him out frequently—like we all should do—especially after he eats or drinks. But when the dog gets a little older but is still a puppy, I take their face in my hands and say: "This is your home too and we want to keep it nice and you can help me keep it nice by not being destructive." Laugh if you want, but it works and many people didn't believe the dogs could be trained this way until two people that live with me saw it work. No one can tell me they are not cognitive and I give rewards for a job well done, but more than a treat—the real treat is your presence and your attention and love.

This next story tells about how a cat protected a man from a very dangerous situation by warning him with the psychic sense and knowledge that there was danger nearby. Melissa writes, "When I was a young girl, my dad was working outside one day moving a pile of bricks. Every time he reached down to pick up a brick, our cat would try to scratch his hand. He thought the cat just wanted some attention, but he came to find out that there was a snake under the pile of bricks and the cat had kept him from getting bitten by the snake. Thank God for that cat."

This is another story that shows animals know things before we do—or in this case, even before a doctor knows. Ana writes, "I have a small mix terrier dog that I got in college. Austin has really been with me through thick and thin, and we share a strong bond. About a year after I got married, Austin started jumping on me, putting his front feet on each side of me (kind of one on each hip), and nudging and sniffing my tummy. This was definitely bizarre behavior from him, as he had never done anything like that before, and he wasn't one for jumping too much. He continued this for about a week, nudging and sniffing my tummy as often as he could.

"After a while I really started wondering what in the world he was doing when a little light came on inside my head, and I decided that I might want to take a pregnancy test, even though I wasn't showing any other symptoms of pregnancy. Sure enough, I was pregnant, and Austin was the first to know."

This next story shows a dear pet who knew what was going to happen—this is a classic example of precognitive knowledge, but it also represents a strong protective instinct on the part of an animal on behalf of her owner. We'll talk about these kinds of animal bravery and protection stories again later in the book, but this story in particular shows how an animal's psychic ability in the immediate *now* prevented her owner from being harmed.

Maria writes: "I would like to tell you about my little poodle Kajsa. We were going for a walk and we were about to cross a road, we had a green light and I started walking, but Kajsa did not move. I pulled the leash, but she refused to budge.

"Then suddenly I saw a car coming, and the driver was looking elsewhere and did not notice that he had a red light, so he kept going. If Kajsa hadn't stopped me, we both would have been run over. The driver didn't even stop to see if we were okay. Kajsa saved my life that time."

In reading many of the stories in which an animal showed a psychic ability, I noticed how many stories included an ability or a feeling that was immediate—and sometimes fleeting—like the story above with Maria and her dog. Being a psychic I am constantly getting feelings and impressions (unless I tone it down a bit and tune them out). These feelings are usually regarding the future (and to a lesser degree the past, if I'm asked a specific question). But rarely will I get a psychic impression that has to have an immediate resolution, such as Maria's dog stopping dead in its tracks and refusing to move to keep Maria and herself out of danger. This is truly a special manifestation.

The more I thought about it, the more I became convinced that the psychic abilities in animals are more pronounced than in humans when the abilities activate due to urgency. Animals don't think about their feelings; they just manifest what they feel is the appropriate behavior to those feelings. Humans, on the other hand, might get an impression of danger and sit there mulling it over in their mind and asking themselves why they are feeling this way. Animals are much more instinctual, and being less complicated in nature, they just react immediately to the psychic feelings they are getting—whether it's danger, protection, love, and so on.

Animals Are Healers

I'm convinced that animals are natural healers, but more than that, science is beginning to show that they can also detect maladies at the early stages. Doctors are now using dogs for the diagnosis of cancer and other illnesses. They feel that when a person has cancer they give off a different odor that only a dog can detect. I'm sure it's as if they can smell if there are drugs being smuggled into an airport and we as humans don't have that advanced sense of smell or hearing or eyesight for that matter. It's as if they can be guardians to help us in this world that seems confusing and dark to us. They are here to help and aid us along the path of life. I believe animals have the ability to assimilate negative energy, depression, and many other illnesses that have not been explored. Perhaps one day science will realize the true healing properties of these angels on earth.

In fifty-four years of readings, I've heard and seen how dogs help us in a variety of different situations, but in particular I've learned how they can use their energy to actually heal the people they love. Because they are directly infused beings from God, they are embodied with extraordinary gifts. This next story is only one example of the many dogs I've seen and heard of that heal mental illness, chronic stomach problems, headaches, anxiety, and so on.

Meghan writes: "My mom has a heart condition that causes her heart to beat irregularly. A few years ago, my mom had been stuck in a vicious 'cycle' of her heart problem for three days and couldn't see how to get out of it. One evening while we were watching TV, my dog Shasta (who *always* sits on my lap) got up, walked over to my mom Wendy (who was lying down), jumped up onto her chest, and just sat there for about five minutes. This was out of the norm for Shasta as she is a *very* hyper dog.

"When Shasta jumped off and walked back to me, my mom sat up and in shock had me check her heart rate—sure enough it was back to normal."

I just want to bring the reader up to the

level of understanding that our pets are not just cute little balls of fur. We would realize this more if we would only observe our pets more closely. Most people do, but sometimes we just don't pay attention, and I've even been guilty of this myself with my dogs.

In writing about animals and illness, this next story shows how anmals sense this and who could be trained to do this. Sometimes even doctors miss what a dog or cat senses. Melissa writes, "One night I came home from playing darts and I had stayed out later than usual. I went right to bed. I woke up with Smokie, my blue Russian cat, partly lying on me with one paw over my neck/chest, and Callie, my other cat, sitting on my chest. I thought it was kind of weird, as they only lie on me when I'm sick. I went back to sleep, and probably an hour later I woke up again—they were still sitting on me. But this time, I felt very weird and was shaking all over. Then it hit me: I had forgotten to take my medication when I came home, and I was going through withdrawal. (That happens if I don't take it on time every night.) Somehow, even before I did, they knew and stood by me to try and let me know."

The one who tells the stories rules the world.
—HOPI

Just as animals can have a sixth sense about illness and other physical changes, they can also help us to heal and alleviate our pain. They just neutralize it, without absorbing it. Rhawnie writes, "I am a dog person, the bigger and 'dumber' the better. Cats know this and for the most part are not really drawn to me. I am a little allergic to cats and as lovable as some of them are, my totem (a tiger) is the only cat I am truly connected to. When I was going through puberty, in fact until I had my first child, I used to have the worst menstrual cramps. It's in the genes; all the women in my family have had it bad at one time or another, and as I don't really like taking more medicines than necessary, I usually would just take a couple of Tylenol to take the edge off.

"Being a teenager I, of course, spent the night at my friend's house at least once a month. She had this gorgeous mahogany/ black male cat named "Blackie." He pretty much kept to himself, but was very sweet when you would pet him or talk to him. Every night he slept with my friend in her bed, but whenever I spent the night and I was menstruating, that cat would refuse to sleep with my friend and would instead curl up on my lower abdomen and purr like crazy all night. The first time we thought he was confused, but no matter what my friend did he would not stay in bed with her. After a couple of tries, I told her not to worry about it and that if he wanted to sleep so badly on my stomach he was welcome to.

"Well, we should've known better than to underestimate Blackie. Within about twenty minutes of him purring loudly on my abs, my cramps were gone. Sure, Blackie was a male and I was essentially 'in heat,' but I have always treated animals with the utmost respect and I have always believed that they held many powers, one, of course, being healing. I don't doubt for one minute that Blackie knew exactly what he was doing, and though any other given night he was snuggled deep with my friend, during those times of the month, even if my friend was suffering the same woes (albeit less painful), that cat was right on top of my abdomen."

Some stories I grant you can be coincidental or a little bit more ordinary, but all of them, whether dramatic or not, have a common thread of knowing—animals somehow know about illness, danger, or even know when to intervene to stop a terrible mishap. It's this sentient, some might even say psychic, ability of pets to understand what we need, and somehow provide it to us that is so powerful. Out of thousands of letters and e-mails, it's impossible, no matter what grid of statistics you use, to not realize the evidence of this "humanized" behavior on the part of the animals we love—humanized in the sense of either precognition, or protection, or just plain psychic sense (seeing loved ones who have passed). And this is not just true of the rescue dog or guard dog that has been trained to find drugs or buried bodies. I'm talking about your pets—the ones that live and love you and are part of your family without training to warn or to do medical diagnosis.

This next story again shows how dogs

have tremendous ESP. As Judy writes, "On August 14, 2006, my mother-in-law was very ill. She had just been brought home from the hospital, and I had just completed an e-mail to my friends and family updating them about her condition. All of a sudden, all three of my Maltese dogs jumped into my lap. They would not leave me alone; all three were standing up on me, kissing my face, and they were very anxious for some odd reason. They all lay down on my lap and closed their eyes.

"Just then the phone rang—it was my husband informing me his mother had passed away. I knew right there and then that our dogs knew that their 'grandma' had passed away. I am a believer that animals have that sixth sense, and they knew she was leaving for the Other Side. They loved her unconditionally and she loved them."

Her dogs did know about the passing of her mother-in-law because they were very psychic and were trying to give her solace. As with these stories and the ones that follow, how could we not believe on a logical level that these animals are not pure entities, almost like guardian angels that are here to protect us and give us comfort

and solace. It also shows that they understand and have reasoning and comprehend
problems we don't even know about, and I
feel that we haven't even scratched the
surface of their knowledge. I'm also convinced that they have a language that is
only understood by them. They have proved
that dolphins can communicate by the
change in their high-pitched whistles. Why
not our four-legged God-sent animals?

This reminds me of some incidents when
I taught school (I was a schoolteacher for
eighteen years), but still did psychic readings. There was a boy named Juan in my
fourth grade class who suffered from terrible seizures. The school let Juan bring a
dog, Brutus, to class, and Brutus would
just lie on the floor all day, unless Juan
was in danger of a seizure. Right before
Juan was going to have a seizure, Brutus
would let out a low guttural sound. Then
we would run and hold Juan, call the nurse,
and keep him from biting his tongue.
Somehow, Brutus had an ability to sense
an oncoming seizure and gave us the
warning we needed to protect Juan. This
was thirty years ago, so we weren't as
medically advanced as we are now, but

Brutus certainly loved and protected his master Juan.

A friend of mine takes a couple of her dogs to visit the elderly, and as soon as her pups enter the home the residents immediately light up. There was one elderly lady she worked with who hadn't said a word to the nursing staff in months—until my friend brought her cocker spaniel. The interesting part is that out of all the residents present in the room that day, her dog went directly to this older woman and jumped on her lap. At first the woman just sat there, and then slowly one hand came up and began to pet the dog. The dog licked her hand and, wonder of wonders, in front of the whole staff she said, "good dog." The staff was just blown away, and it shows how animals have the ability to heal and dispel negativity and even open the part of the limbic brain that responds to unconditional love.

Man has responsibility, not power.
—TUSCARORA

Another young woman I know has a shepherd-mix dog. She also works with autistic children. One day she brought the dog to work with her, and all the children who seemed isolated and locked inside of themselves immediately came over to pet the dog. She said that day she got more response from the children than she had the whole time she had worked with these children. The school then let her bring her dog every day, and the way these children opened up was no less than miraculous.

The following stories are written by the same person who had two dogs that are examples of the unsung heroes of this world. In the first story the dog wasn't going to let her go anywhere until she made sure her husband was alright, as he had for her. Dee writes, "We rescued a puppy that's Rottweiler/bull mastiff mix six years ago. We named her Kobe, and other than barking way too much, she's brought us immense joy. The first night we had her, she sat in her crate and *howled* until I finally gave in and put her next to my chest so she could hear my heart beat. No more crying, no messes in the bed, so, of course, that's where she slept from then on.

"I have diabetes, and on two different occasions, she woke me up and kept nagging me until I gave in and checked my blood sugar. Both times, it was low and I needed to go get some juice. One other time, she had trouble getting me awake and by the time I did wake up, my blood sugar was so low I couldn't get up. Kobe realized that I was in trouble and went into my husband's bedroom and woke him up. By the time she got him to realize there was something wrong, I was starting to slip into unconsciousness. He was able to get enough juice poured down me, along with a lot down my front, that I was able to 'come to.'

"As if that wasn't enough, one night Kobe was barking and yipping and almost tearing my bedroom door down. I was reluctant to get up because I was really tired so she started jumping on my bed and licking me roughly and then back to the door, back to the bed, and back to the door. I decided to give in, opened up the door, and started down the hall to open the back door. However, Kobe got in front of me and stopped me. She started 'herding' me toward my husband's bedroom. She went to his door and started the barking, yipping, and trying to open the door routine again. I heard a strange noise but I just assumed it was his sleep apnea machine. I started to go back to bed but she wouldn't let me. She pushed me back toward Mike's room again, and I opened up his door so she could sleep with him. As I did this, I realized the noise was Mike gagging. He had been battling a bad cold. It turned out he had influenza and pneumonia and he was aspirating because the machine was forcing all the 'gunk' back into his throat. As soon as I yanked off the mask, Kobe immediately became quiet and calm so I could work on him without any interference. I sat him up and pounded out as much of the gunk as possible. When the ER doctor looked at him, it turned out that Mike had also had a heart attack. The doc told me that another fifteen minutes would have cost Mike his life.

"Our rescued pup became the rescuer (and hero). Since that night, she has chosen to sleep at the intersecting halls—between our bedrooms so she can keep an eye on both of us."

This next story is again one of disease detection by an animal, but this one is exceptional. Janet writes, "In late 2004, my sixteen-year-old Jellico cat began jumping upon my father's lap and sitting atop his stomach and continued to do this for about two months and then began putting his mouth up to my father's as if he was smelling his breath.

"Approximately six months later my father was diagnosed with pancreatic cancer and given only ten months to live. Shortly after my cat began sitting right on top of his stomach, we found out later that he was sitting in the area of the pancreas. After Domino (my cat) began sitting on this area is when my father started having problems and went to the doctor. The first doctor would not do any tests and just told him it was acid reflux and to treat it with meds. Finally, he kept having more and more pain, and the cat would not leave his stomach area every time he sat down. We took him to another doctor. They did one CAT scan and there was the cancer already too far advanced to operate. He went through the chemo and radiation, but he was just diagnosed too late. If we would have paid attention to Domino my father might be here today. Domino himself passed at the age of eighteen in May of 2007. He is with my father, this I know . . ."

These next two stories are also about the caring and sentient knowledge that our pets have—to see and sense and give comfort and even heal. Think about it— only a being with intelligence can do these things, not just a "dumb animal," which again I so sorely resent. As I have said, there are so many stories that I received about pets and animals, but I hope these shared stories give knowledge to those who don't know about animals and give comfort and insight to those of us who do.

Kris writes: "Three years ago my lupus had worsened and I had another mystery illness that the doctor thought was something called valley fever. Apparently, it is from a spore in the southwest United States, although I hadn't been there. I had tremendous fatigue, swelling, and rashes. Although it was a hot summer, I could not get warm.

"One afternoon, lying on the couch under three quilts, I could feel the life force leaving me. I knew I was going to die and

I was ready, simply because I was so tired of steroids, chemo, thirteen prescription drugs, and feeling worse every day. I was only fifty-two years old. My cat, who is not a snuggly cat, insisted on crawling under the covers and draping himself over my body. I drifted off and was surprised when I woke up alive.

"I returned to the doctor. I was suffering from hypothermia due to a nonfunctioning thyroid, something they hadn't thought to check. I know my cat kept me warm enough to live through the day I thought would be my last. I've also noticed that my unfriendly cat who hides from visitors in my home will always snuggle up to a visitor who is suffering from a serious illness. If my cat Rascal cuddles up to you, it's time to get a complete physical.

"Because of this unusual experience, I began to explore alternative medicine. I'm happy to report that I no longer have thirteen prescriptions, just thyroid medication and hormone replacement. I found a great homeopathic healer and the lupus I suffered for eighteen years is gone. Another unusual thing my Rascal does is sense my down days. I've had many over the past several months because we lost everything in a fire. On my bad days, he'll jump on my lap, put his paw gently on my face, and stare into my eyes as if to reassure me that things will work out eventually. It's the only time he does this.

"My cat opened a door to another world. The journey also led me to a spiritual rebirth and a letting go of early childhood trauma, which I believe was manifesting as an autoimmune disease. Every form of healing has its place, and God gives us healers in many forms. They don't all graduate from medical school."

The following story tells about a pet rabbit that saved its owner's life and possibly that of her unborn child at the time. Darcy writes, "I am writing my submission to your request for amazing animal stories. Most people have stories about cats and dogs, but our story is about our rabbit, Robin. Here it is:

"My name is Darcy. I live with my husband, Edward, and at the time this story took place we had two children, Callie, age ten, and Dylan, age eight. We live in the country near Port Byron, Illinois. We had talked for a long time about getting a pet rabbit for the family. Well, I was about eight months pregnant with our third child at the time, and with a new baby coming we really felt that we should wait awhile before purchasing such a responsibility. As fate would have it, there was another plan in store for us! While I was out going to garage sales one day in April of 2005, I came across a sale out in the middle of the country. While looking for good bargains I discovered that the family having the garage sale had bunnies for sale. I thought, no, I better not even look because we had decided that now was not the time. However, I went and looked at them anyway. There were a few of them left and they were so adorable that I asked if I could hold one of them. So, I picked one up and that was it! I bought him, for a whole ten dollars! On the way home I called my husband and warned him of the news. When I got home and showed the kids they were ecstatic! So, although this was not the plan (or so we thought), that bunny ended up saving my life and my baby's life.

"We had had the ten-week-old bunny for about three weeks and he was *so* good! He was very quiet and kept to himself and was very easy to take care of. He never made any noise. He would let us pet him, but really did not like to sit still. We kept him in a cage in the living room that consisted of a big Rubbermaid container with a lid made out of chicken wire that we had thrown together to make sure he did not get out.

"Well, as I stated earlier, I was pregnant with our third child due in June. I had had gestational diabetes with my second pregnancy but it was diet controlled. This time I was on insulin, a lot of insulin. Each time I went to the doctor they kept having to increase my dosage because it was just not staying under control very well. It was a very difficult pregnancy to say the least! Well, on the night of Friday, May 13, 2005, everything was normal as usual. The kids went upstairs to bed around 9:00 p.m. and my husband and I went to bed shortly thereafter. I should note that usually I am the light sleeper and my husband could sleep through a tornado, not hearing anything being such a sound sleeper.

"At about three in the morning my husband woke up to our usually quiet bunny rabbit in the living room making quite the racket. He was jumping up and scratching, trying vigorously to get out of the cage, which he had *never* done before. So my husband, the usually sound sleeper, got out of bed to try and quiet the bunny down so that I could sleep. He petted the bunny for awhile and tried to calm him down and after a little while it worked. So my husband went back to bed. Very soon after, the bunny started right back up making so much noise. Once again my husband got up to quiet the bunny down to make sure he would not wake anyone else in the house. He could not figure out what was wrong with the bunny because the bunny was so persistent about jumping up and down and making his lid go up and down to make a loud noise. He was just scratching the side walls and doing everything he could to be loud, which he had never done before. Finally, the rabbit quieted down again and my husband decided to sleep on the couch next to the rabbit just in case he did it again.

"Before lying back down though, he thought he heard me in our room having a bad dream. So he came and checked on me to wake me up from my bad dream so that I could try to go back to sleep again. When he came into our room, he couldn't get me to wake up so he turned on the light. To his surprise my eyes were wide open and rolled back into my head and I was completely unresponsive! He immediately dialed 911 and told the operator that his wife was not responding. In the process of talking to her he remembered that my gestational diabetes instructor had told him that if I was ever not responding well to put cake frosting in the sides of my cheek to get sugar to me faster. So he put the phone down and ran right to the refrigerator and got the frosting, which just happened to be on the top shelf where he immediately saw it and grabbed it (we never keep frosting in the refrigerator)! He then proceeded to explain to the operator that I was a gestational diabetic. My husband was very scared as we live in the country and only have a volunteer emergency response team and thought it might take a long time to get to me. As it turns out though, our volunteer emergency response team had literally just finished going to another call (at 3:00 a.m. in the morning) in which a man had diabetes, and he lived right down the same road as we did!

"When they got to our house my blood sugar was down to 22—I had gone into a diabetic coma! They gave me a shot of something (we are still unsure what exactly it was) which brought me back, and then took me to the hospital. I ended up spending five days in the hospital to get my blood sugar under control. For some unknown reason, my blood sugar just kept going up and up and then one night just completely dropped to a life-threatening level!

"I went on to have the baby on June 13, a healthy baby girl named Brenna Violet Marie.

"So many things lined up just right for us that night—the frosting being in the refrigerator right where we could find it, the ambulance being down the same road at that time of the morning, and especially that new little bunny who was *so very* insistent on waking someone up to notice that I had gone into a diabetic coma. We know that God was very much with us that night and used our bunny as a means to get our attention to take action! If I hadn't decided to buy that bunny at that garage sale we don't know what could have happened.

"I should note that we really spoil that bunny now, whose name is Robin, and also interestingly we feel that the bunny has a very strong connection with Brenna, our youngest child, whose life the bunny played a very big role in. We notice this by the fact that Brenna is the only one who Robin will let pick up and carry around with her, sit very still for her, and come to her if he is running around.

"We know that there are dogs and other animals out there that can detect seizures and such, but we definitely feel that our bunny has amazing capabilities and picked up on the sensation of the drop in my blood sugar level. If it weren't for Robin, we might have had a different result. We are very blessed and thankful that this bunny was put in our lives for this very special reason!"

6

GRIEF AND ANIMALS—
OURS AND THEIRS

"Life is not separate from death. It only looks that way."
—Blackfoot Indian proverb

Do animals feel emotional pain and grief? Anyone who has loved an animal knows that the range of their pet's emotions—from joy to confusion to sadness—is as diverse and real as ours. Animals not only feel emotional pain but they are also sensitive to pain in the humans they love, and will do anything in their power to alleviate our suffering. In this chapter we'll hear amazing tales of animals' emotions, from the empathy they show one another to the love they show for us when we need it the most.

Animals Grieve

African elephants have a wonderful social structure that is basically matriarchal in nature. All male elephants after a certain age are excluded from the herd, but the way the females care for their young and their elderly, and particularly their grief when one of the herd is lost, is something to behold. In those situations, the group's sadness is palpable; they keep trying to get the dying elephant up on its feet while the herd stands in a protective circle as if to keep watch. You can actually see and feel their anguish. I watched a scene like this, and one of the huge elephants who was the matriarch trumpeted in a way I'll never forget—it was a pure cry of pain.

In this next story, we can see a closer-to-home example of how animals grieve. Debra writes, "My daughter has always been an animal lover; many times throughout her childhood she would bring home a stray of one kind or another. When she was around ten years old, her beautiful rambunctious black Lab was spending the day in the kennel behind our house. My daughter let 'Sady' out for some exercise. The dog went to the end of the woods, where it came across a baby bunny rabbit. Unfortunately, the dog did not realize it would hurt the bunny and started playing with it far too forcefully. My daughter, realizing that Sady had inadvertently harmed the bunny, wrapped it in a towel and came in the house crying. But try as I might, I could not save the rabbit.

"We took the bunny outside to bury it, and upon saying our prayers my daughter put wildflowers on the new grave site. Around two hours later we went outside and the mama rabbit was sitting quietly at the grave site; it was a beautiful spiritual moment. Many times people say animals do not have a spirit or are incapable of feeling, but after the rabbit experience I no longer believe this. It has been several years since this incident, and wildflowers continue to grow in the very spot where we buried the baby rabbit."

All animals grieve. Several years ago, one of my two beloved Lhasa Apsos died. The two dogs were siblings, raised together since birth, and they had never been apart. Mitsy, my surviving dog, went under the bed to grieve, and no matter how I coaxed her she wouldn't come out to play, drink, or eat. Finally an idea dawned on me, and I immediately got another Lhasa Apso puppy that was as close to the markings that I could get of Chewy who had died.

The minute I brought the new puppy inside, Mitsy poked her head out from under the bed and began to watch the puppy. After about two hours she came out and began to play with him. She might have thought her beloved brother had shrunk even though she probably knew the difference, but somehow, it just didn't matter. From that day on, just like before, they were inseparable. The only thing that seemed different is that Mitsy was extra protective of the next Chewy. I guess she was afraid she might lose him again.

We humans are not the only ones that have a heart, mind, and soul that feels grief, hurt, and regret. If we know this, then why wouldn't we understand that animals feel loneliness, abandonment, and grief just like we do? I don't ever want to address the cruelty and even the experiments that are done on animals, because for one thing I can't bear it and it haunts me for days. I just hope that eventually by educating people and with enough voices raised in protest, we will stop this brutal treatment of these marvelous beings that have done nothing but help and often save us.

Don't be afraid to cry. It will free your mind of sorrowful thoughts.
—HOPI

Animals Comfort Us

The stories of spirit animals coming back to visit are innumerable. My friend lost her beloved poodle and after his death she actually saw him in the front room just standing and looking at her. He looked so real she was ready to go over and hug him and then he was gone.

Another woman wrote that her cat used to sleep on her head at night and wrap his tail under her chin. After his passing she was lying there one night and felt the cat jump on the bed. She thought she was just imagining it until she felt the pressure on her head and felt the furry tail under her chin. She even reached up and for a few seconds actually felt the tail and then it was gone. Her sweet cat came back to say, *See, I still exist, and I will always be with you, and even more important I will be waiting for you.* This next story also shows this.

Zanda writes, "About a month or two ago, I was listening to the radio when I heard a commercial with a man talking about how to train your pets. It got me thinking about how smart my dog had been. He was just a puppy when I got him on my birthday when I was in the sixth grade, and he died on Mother's Day more than thirty years ago.

"I was thinking about him and missing him terribly. A few days later, I went to bed and dozed off with my left arm stretched out on the bed. All of a sudden I felt a long lick up the inside of my left arm. It felt like a wet tongue. I opened my eyes and felt my arm but it was dry.

"I was not even thinking about my dog that night. But I know it must have been him. A human spirit is not going to come around and lick your arm—unless it is a little on the kinky side! I do believe that it was my dog saying hello. I miss him; it is comforting to know that he is alive and well on the Other Side."

I know when you lose a pet the grief is real and raw. However, as time goes on and the hurt subsides, we can be grateful that we were blessed with their presence. Pet lovers all remember how much our beloved animals gave us, and how much better life was because we had the grace to know them and love them. Then, as we loved them and they loved us in return, a spiritual and loving connection was made, and because of this we will be reunited with them for eternity. After all, life is so transient for all of us, and some are never blessed with the love of a loyal and protective pet.

These experiences remind us that we must look at this transient world as a plane that we are just passing through, and rather than running through the beauty around us stressed and worried about everything, we should be happy for this beauty—the trees, animals, mountains, family, and friends in our lives. We're here on this earth for such a short time (even if we live to be a hundred), and before we know it we will be back home on the Other Side, in a beautiful meadow romping with our pets and loved ones. We can't live like this world is all there is to creation because it definitely isn't, and this existence was never meant to be the true reality of life.

This next letter is from a real animal lover who has had several experiences with her pets visiting her. This story also addresses the question of euthanasia and when it is more merciful to let your animal go rather than keep him or her hanging on in pain and suffering in this life. To experience the death of one of your beloved pets is extremely difficult, but even though we love them we must also take the responsibility to end any horrible suffering that they are going through for their sake. Although most pets that have passed will visit from time to time, they do not become earthbound like some humans do, but sometimes (as put forth in the following story) they will hang around after dying. You can then tell them to go home to the Other Side like Sandy did, because they will always be waiting for you when you eventually pass over.

Sandy writes, "About a decade ago, I had a cat (long haired, black and white) called Crazy (she earned her name as a small kitten). She was thirteen years old when she developed a health problem, and I had to make the awful decision to put her to sleep. It was a horrible ordeal (not my first and it won't be my last, as animals always will be in my life). Crazy always lay on the railing of my water bed every night before I fell asleep. The day I had her put to sleep, I thought about her constantly, and that night I could hear her purring, right in the same spot she always did. I told my husband to come listen. He even heard it (a nonbeliever!). I searched everywhere to figure out where the 'noise' was coming from. I looked behind the headboard, along the bed, outside the window. The purring was coming directly from the water bed railing. Even my husband (now my ex) *knew* that it was my cat Crazy. There was no doubt. This went on every night for two weeks.

"Finally, I went down to my beautiful little pet cemetery in the nearby woods, a beautiful little place with multiple cats and two dogs. I always did talk to my animals, but that night I directed my words at Crazy. I said I knew she was here with me and that

I loved her. I then told her it was okay, she could 'go' and I would see her later.

"Crazy never came back to my bed railing again. I do miss her, but I do know I will be greeted by *many* more animals than human spirits when I cross over."

Old age is not as honorable as death, but most people want it.
—CROW

Susan tells a similar story: "I had to put my one dog, Toots, to sleep. He suffered a horrible death. By the time I found out he had blastomycosis, he already could barely breathe and he had lost a lot of weight. One night as he lay on 'his' couch, I talked to him and told him to please give me a sign as to when I should let him go. Within minutes, he started gasping and coughing. I knew this was my sign. So I made an emergency trip to the vet at 5:00 a.m. and helped my beloved black Lab/basset cross over to the Other Side.

"I brought him home and buried him myself. Later that day I could hear his collar jingle like it always did. I did not bury his collar with him; it was hanging up on my dresser. I have since caught glimpses of him throughout my house. In the beginning I do believe I caught him on film sitting next to his beloved cat, Treelo, who I still have. I do occasionally feel my cats and dogs rub up against my legs. I can tell the difference if they are a cat or dog." It can be tough to let our pets go, but knowing that they have crossed over and are happy on the Other Side is a great comfort to many of us.

This next story is self-explanatory, and, of course, Sophie grieves and knows. Debra writes, "My dog, Sophie the schnauzer, is ten years old. She was only one hour old when I met her. Her mother, Midge, was seventeen when she had to be put to sleep last September after a long and wonderful life. I own Sophie, but her mother Midge stayed with us much of the time when her humans were out of town. They became more than friends and actually were more like twins.

"The day that Midge was put to sleep, my dog Sophie suddenly 'became' her mother. She never saw the remains and she hasn't been back to the other humans' house since. For over a month, Sophie *was* her mother Midge—not being able to go up the stairs, having to be carried, staring into a corner, and every other trait of the older mother. She has now come back to her old self. My question is, and I already know the answer, how did Sophie *know* that her mother was gone?"

Strange as it sounds, it's actually possible for the spirit of a pet to inhabit another animal's body, just as Midge did with Sophie. Because of the close psychic bond between the two animals, Sophie felt Midge's death particularly strongly.

Many years ago, we had a dachshund named Suzie who would chase cars. She didn't bark at them; she just chased them. We had her fenced and tried everything, but she still would somehow crawl out and chase cars.

One morning when I was driving the kids to school, we were all talking and laughing until we heard a thump. I instantly got sick to my stomach and thought to myself, *Oh dear God, I just know I ran over Suzie*. Sure enough I had run over her, but the car had just caught her right leg. I immediately took Suzie to the vet. He said she would live but he'd have to amputate the leg. "A dog with only three legs—you should put her to sleep," he said. I asked him if he had lost an arm, should we put him to sleep? He looked at me for awhile and then he said, "I see how you feel." Suzie came home with us that night.

Even with three legs she got along fine, and she lived to be fifteen years old; she was very active, and you could hear her distinctive gait throughout the house. Long after she died I could hear her clump around in the kitchen and down the hall. She was checking in to see how we all were. So no one can ever tell me that love of our dear pets, as all true love, doesn't survive death.

We Grieve for Our Animals

There is nothing that can completely stop or staunch the anguish we feel when we lose a loved one or a beloved pet, but to know they are waiting for us on the Other Side is such a comfort. Please don't feel bad or guilty when you grieve for your pets that have passed over. It's natural, but it's not a helpful emotion.

When my dog Misty died, the worst part about her death was that a coyote got her. I had all the feelings so many of you have related to me: *Could I have done more? Why did I leave her out alone that night? Why didn't I check to see if she was in the dog run with the other dogs?* But you can't let that kind of guilt take hold of you— remember you are here to experience life, not to regret it. When I found Misty she had been viciously attacked by a wild animal. I found myself screaming, blood was every- where, and she was hardly breathing. But she looked up at me with such love. I kept saying, "I'm sorry darling, I'm so sorry and I love you." She closed her eyes and died.

While I was holding Misty, I saw a white filmlike substance that came right out of her body and formed into an outline of her. Then across my lawn I saw a gold light that looked like a miniature sun. The outline of Misty ran toward it, and as she did the light turned brilliant white. I could see a figure standing beside it that was definitely an angel. Misty ran right into the white light and I saw the figure reach down and pick her up, and then everything was dark again.

I sat on the step holding her dead body, and even though I had been crying hysterically a feeling of such peace came over me. I knew she was alright and God had sent an angel to take her. Sometimes angels come to greet our animals, and sometimes they just go through the light and meet all "their" loved ones and other animals on their own. I know she is with Thor and Buddy and Crystal and Mindy and Heathcliff (one of my cats) and Jolie and Lance and all the pets I've had and lost through all my seventy-two years.

I buried Misty in the backyard. The next day I looked out and saw all the dogs circled around the grave site. Not only did they know she was gone but they were giving love and homage to some entity they knew and loved. Troy, who was so close to her, sat in the flower bed all day and wouldn't come out. I knew what it was; it was grief. In fact, that whole week after, all my pets were quiet and off their food. They knew that they had lost the little frisky pest that used to nibble their ears and run around in circles to entertain all of them.

About two weeks later, I swore I heard her bark (anyone who has pets can tell whose bark belongs to what dog), and as I ran outside my other dogs were all looking at one spot in the yard. The grass was wet from the sprinklers and it was fairly long because the gardener had not come yet. As I looked where they were staring I could see the grass go down in a circle, which is what she would do—run in a circle to get them to play. All my dogs ran to where the circle was and began to play. I said to myself, *dear God they see her and are playing with her spirit*, a presence that seemed as real to them as if she was really there.

This doesn't mean that dogs are ever ghosts; no, they are spirits that come back and visit just like many of our passed over loved ones do. Misty would show up fairly often for a time, and she still does (but less frequently, as she is too busy playing with other animals and running through the lush meadows of the Other Side).

Why would thousands have these experiences if they weren't true? Why would thousands of people like you and me just tune into some imaginary tale, which is what religion and society say we do? The answer is simple—we don't. Society and religion feel that they are on pretty solid ground when they deal with an individual experience, but that quickly becomes like quicksand when you throw thousands of paranormal experiences at them. You who have had these experiences and are afraid to relate them—don't be. You are certainly not alone, and thousands of people just like you have had similar experiences. You certainly are not crazy, and it certainly is not your imagination. These manifestations do exist.

Seek wisdom, not knowledge.
Knowledge is of the past,
Wisdom is of the future.
—LUMBEE

In my research I've found through the thousands of hypnosis regressions, near death experiences, dreams, and astral travel experiences of thousands of subjects from every culture, race, ethnic background, and country, that they all relate the same way or have very similar experiences with spirits, contact with passed over loved ones or pets, and the Other Side. They all see or experience basically the same things when it comes to seeing passed over loved ones—the tunnel leading to the Other Side, the bright light, and even viewing glimpses of what the Other Side is like.

It is the same with those who have had experiences with animals and pets. The feelings and experiences of communication and understanding cut through the erroneous belief of "dumb animal," whether it happens in reality or in spirit form. This might seem radical, but sometimes I think we are the ones who are unaware and thick-headed.

The reason I have included this next story (it is long) is because it illustrates another type of grief—the anguish we feel when animals take actions we can't understand. There is so much controversy about pit bulls, who at times can act almost schizophrenic—sweet one moment and dangerous the next. It's my fervent belief that they are not evil and they can't help themselves. Their sometimes erratic behavior is man's fault from years of inbreeding; they instinctively want to fight and to grab and hold on. They can be the sweetest dogs (I know, I had one), and one day it's as if something clicks in their head. One vet I spoke to said it's like a child going through puberty—one day he is fine and the next day he becomes a different person. So it is with pit bulls—it's an inbred defect that is not their fault. It's man's fault. Humankind can't be content, it seems, to leave nature alone. But God knows what creation should be, we don't, and time will prove that.

But pit bulls can be dangerous. Anyone, especially anyone who has children, should consider carefully and do their research before taking in a pit bull for a pet. Like poor Sara in this story found out, they can change their normal disposition in a heartbeat. The trials and tribulations that Sara and her fiancé are going through will only make both of them stronger, and we must always remember that God doesn't heap woe upon us—we each write our trials into our own life Chart.

Nevertheless, we can empathize with the grievous feelings of Sara as she writes, "My fiancé got Thor, a pure white English Striker pit bull, about two weeks before he met me. Even when we went through tough times, John and I always said 'as long as we have each other, we'll be okay,'" and that 'each other' included Thor. He was our baby boy, our joy, our happiness. We always felt love, even if we were battered in everything else. Our friends and family would tease us and say we treated our dog like he was our child.

"I gave Thor a bunch of stuffed animals for Christmas two years ago. He got an ostrich 'Big Bird,' an armadillo 'Dillo,' a mallard 'Duckie,' a whale 'Whallee,' along with a baby blue Easter duckie 'Blue Duckie.' Thor loved each of them—he would take 'Dillo' outside and set him upright and roll his tennis ball to him. He thought those 'babies,' as we called them, were real, at least real enough to play with. In a sense, they were his babies.

"Every night at bedtime we had a routine. He would give his Daddy good-night kisses, then me good-night kisses, then I would tuck him in bed. A very structured process. I would kneel down and straighten his blankets, he would then climb in the middle, and if cold I would cover him. Then Thor would lie sideways and I would give him 'Dillo' to spoon with. All of his other babies would be strategically positioned around him. Once everyone was tucked in, I would bend over and give Thor a good night kiss. He would squirm a little and give me the *Mommy, I love you so much* look and I would scratch him under his chin, get up, and go to bed. Every night we did this. John, my fiancé, would just laugh and say how spoiled Thor was. I never worried though; I knew he appreciated every bit of it.

"One night, while I was visiting my mother with Thor, I changed into my nightclothes, brushed my teeth, and so on, and then went into my room to perform Thor's 'tucking in' ritual. Kisses, then blanket fluffing, he crawled in, no covers since it was hot, I gave him Dillo, which he spooned. He looked at me, cuddled Dillo, gave me the Mommy, I love you so much look—and then it happened.

"For whatever reason that night I did not bend over to kiss him as usual, instead I just scratched him under his chin. When I backed up to stand up, he growled just a little and snapped down on my hand that I was still pulling away from his chin. As I did not process what was happening I tried pulling my hand from his mouth, but again he snapped down but harder this time. Blood flowed from my hand. It was then that I realized that my boy was attacking me. I did not scream, but instead calmly told Thor with tears welling that he was hurting Mommy. I repeated this and then noticed his eyes were completely dilated and black. I don't think Thor was there after that. Animal instinct took over and he became violent. He sat up as more blood flowed and began viciously, yet so quietly ripping through the flesh of my left hand first and then he moved to my right arm. I used my right arm to hold his neck and collar to try and keep him away from my face. I knew if I screamed he would lunge and I would be dead.

"Just as he was thrashing through my right arm I heard my sister walk out of her bedroom. I called calmly to her, yet I know she heard the urgency in my voice. She called back to me, her voice shook with fear. She knew something was terribly wrong. She immediately ran over and began trying to rip Thor off of me. Her screams made enough noise that my parents heard and came running up from their room. Stacy's dog Olive came running in behind Stacy, barking frantically, but when she realized what was happening kept barking but hid under the bed. My mother called 911. My father was the one who finally ripped Thor off of me. All I did was cry and kept wailing 'why would my baby do this to me?'

"I went to the hospital, where my arms became so infected I almost lost them both. Lucky for me I had one of the best hand surgeons around. I was in the hospital for nine days and had three surgeries on both arms and hands. Not only do I still have my life, but my arms are going to be normal in a few more months. It has been a lot of therapy and hard work but it has paid off.

"Sadly, I had Thor put down—the animal control authorities quarantined him for twelve days, then put him down. John and

I have been devastated by this. We have both suffered severe depression, though we are coming slowly out and through this. I still cannot for the life of me understand why Thor did this. Was he mad at me? Did he eat something poisonous that made him attack me? He was the sweetest thing ever. I know he is in heaven now, waiting for the day to see us again. But why would God allow animals to attack, to do evil?"

As you can see, Sara is still traumatized to a certain degree and still in the midst of grief. As I stated earlier, animals are not evil (even though all are instinctual), and in this case the inbreeding caused Thor to just snap. Remember how she said she saw Thor's eyes become blank and dilated? We hear about this with human beings who all of a sudden go on a rampage, but it can also happen to animals.

I know Sara and John are good people, but being human Sara's emotions are overriding her intellect and she feels like she must blame someone. They both are working through a hard time in their lives right now but that will end, and the lessons learned of tolerance, patience, and coming closer together through adversity will stand them in good stead later on in their lives. Even though both of them picked these situations to occur in their Charts, like any human being who goes through adversity and grief we have to remember that in being human we will have the human emotions of despair, grief, and hopelessness at times when times get tough. This is not necessarily being weak, it is just called being human, and God knows and understands this. Just remember that God is all-loving and all-merciful and should never be blamed for negativity that is a by-product of humankind. Unfortunately, God, as well as religion, gets falsely blamed a great deal by humans in the world today. This Earth plane is not for reward, but for learning. Our reward is in our real home on the Other Side and that is eternal.

7

ANIMAL BRAVERY
AND PROTECTION

"The rainbow is a sign from Him who
is in all things."
—Hopi Indian proverb

The heroic deeds of animals are innumerable—the telling of them would take a book unto itself! Our animals are wonderful companions, but they also protect us from danger, as the following stories tell. These types of stories make up the bulk of the letters, e-mails, and testimonials that I receive from readers about their animals. It seems nearly everyone has a tale of their pet's bravery, an incident in which their pet protected them from harm, or a story of a pet's heroic deed. Sometimes these stories are psychic or spiritual in nature; other times they are simply a testament to the strong emotional bonds we have with our pets.

Animals Are Brave

Animals really can protect us—both animals in this world and our beloved animals who reach out to us from beyond the Other Side. My dogs actually ran a prowler out of our backyard once! Amazingly, they didn't make a sound until he was already in the backyard; it was almost as if they were quiet so they could ambush him when he finally entered our property! Gail had a similar experience, further validating the many stories of protection that our beloved pets afford us.

Gail writes, "Bear is a seven-year-old Great Pyrenees/Australian shepherd mix and weighs about 110 pounds. When he was three years old, I had him out very late one night in the backyard on his leash. It was dark, and we live at the end of a country lane with a large horse pasture of several acres (fenced in) behind the house. Bear got behind me and clipped me at the back of my knees with his body, dropping me straight to the ground. He then lay next to me, as close as he could get, and started growling like the Hound of the Baskervilles. It scared the daylights out of me—I could not figure out what was happening.

"Suddenly, in the pasture behind the wooden fence, a man darted out of a hiding place and started sprinting across the field. He slammed into a woodpile and started cursing. Bear just kept up his wolf growls, never leaving my side. My neighbor heard all the noise and released his own dogs (two really ancient old boys, but quite large). As soon as Bear heard the other dogs chasing the prowler, he popped up off the ground, and as soon as I got up he led me quickly to the back door. He refuses to go out to the backyard in the dark to this day. Although it was probably just a prowler seeing what he could find, we will never know; there have been no problems since that time."

It isn't just large dogs that warn or protect—there have even been stories of little Chihuahuas that bark and warn their owners. Sometimes little dogs don't even realize what their size is and want to take on any invader. My Westie and Shiatsu think they are big ferocious dogs, not realizing that they would just be a mouthful for a big dog.

Diane writes, "About three years ago my brother found a little beagle up at our camp. She was sick and he took her to the vet. But he couldn't take her home with him, so he brought her to my house, knowing my two little girls would love to have her. And that they did. She healed and loved the attention and the hugs and kisses. Her name was Gypsy.

"Gypsy was shy and, for a beagle, very quiet. She hardly ever barked. She always slept in the laundry room. One evening about 10:00 p.m. she started barking and barking and my husband went to check on her. He asked me if I could smell something burning. He found that the insulation on our hot water tank (which is in the laundry room) was smoldering and ready to catch fire. If it were not for Gypsy, our house could have easily burned down that night.

"Just last week our beloved Gypsy passed away in her sleep. Our family was devastated. My girls made her beautiful headstones of hearts for her grave. She will *always* be in our hearts and never forgotten."

Rhonda writes, "My dog saved my life and my baby's life. I had just given birth two days before. I was in the kitchen boiling the baby bottles to sterilize them, and the baby started crying. I went upstairs to tend to the baby and totally forgot the pot on the stove. My dog, a German Rottweiler named Rocky, was in the kitchen. He barked and barked and barked. I ignored him because I thought he was just seeing something, but he started jumping on the floor like a cat jumping up and down, barking in front of the stove until I came down and it was lucky that I did. The pot was on fire and I caught it just in time to put it out with little damage. My dog is a massive dog, having the size and build of a Great Dane. He weighs about two hundred pounds so when he jumps it makes a huge bang. I thank God every day that I have that dog and I'm thankful to him, for without him my house would have caught fire."

Kathy writes: "My husband and I found a very tiny puppy in the Dumpster one afternoon and couldn't leave him there to starve. As he grew he became very attached to my husband, and we considered him 'his' dog. (We also had a golden retriever.) We named him Bo-Bo. When Bo-Bo was about a year old, I came home from the grocery store and went around to the passenger side of the car to unload my groceries. He placed himself between my car and my house, barking furiously at me, which was very unusual. Every trip I would make outside for more, he would get between me and the house and bark frantically. After the fourth trip I walked up to him to see what the fuss was about and realized that he had put himself between me and a coiled-up rattlesnake. I went back into the house calling him to go with me to safety. After that incident, he also became *my* dog!"

As I've said before, the phrase "dumb animal" makes me crazy. How would a being that is not sentient know that a rattlesnake was dangerous and warn his owner or that a fire could destroy life and property? Their limbic brain has reasoning, along with pure love and fidelity and loyalty and commitment—most of which are sadly missing in our society today. That's why animals go straight to the Other Side or heaven with no stopovers.

Angela writes: "Our golden retriever Kelsea is a grand old lady now who just turned fourteen. Kelsea is a sweet dog that can be slightly aloof, but she has been known to get herself into mischief. For instance, even though she is fourteen years old and can barely hear, see, or walk, she will cross a busy residential street to try and sneak a dog biscuit out of our neighbor's garage. She knows just the spot where they keep the biscuits for their own dog.

"Even though Kelsea is a danger to herself, a few years ago she did something remarkable to guard the safety of my daughter Sarah, who was about eighteen months at the time. Sarah and I were in the backyard enjoying a beautiful day when I needed to run into the house for a moment. Our backyard is completely fenced in so I felt safe in leaving Sarah for a few moments. When I came back out I was in a dead panic, because Sarah was not in the sandbox and I didn't see her anywhere. I went to the side of the house and realized to my horror that the gate had been left open! I ran out front toward the busy street only to see Kelsea standing between Sarah and the road. Kelsea was gently nudging Sarah on the back and literally herding her back toward the open gate. Kelsea got all the dog biscuits she wanted that day."

If you see no reason for giving thanks, the fault lies in yourself.
—MINQUASS

This next story deals with protection, but also other things. I cannot stress enough to watch, pay attention, and listen to your animal's actions and behavior. J. writes, "My cat Friskie has always been a one-person cat and tolerated everyone else. She was my baby. One night she started to bite my toe and make these unusual sounds. My first thought was she was having a medical problem. She kept this alarm up and kept looking at our bedroom door. At the door was a man trying to get in. My husband got up and went downstairs. The man was downstairs yelling, but fled when he saw John. That morning we found his boots at the back door. We put them outside by the road but no one claimed them. Friskie had never done this before or after that incident.

"Friskie has since left us, but I truly believe that she and our other cat Casey still watch over the house. I also think that they come to me at night. I have cats that sleep with me, but when they are asleep, I feel another cat either jumping on or off my bed. My husband does not. I love my cats and am glad that they still visit."

This was a case in which a cat alerted the family that there was an intruder, but even more important it shows that animals come back and visit just as people do. Their spirits go to heaven, but like our passed loved ones they also come back and visit. It shows that nothing is lost *ever* in God's time.

The next story of a dog named Buster says it all and emphasizes what I've been saying about pets going to the Other Side—Buster will make it to heaven with no problems. They give love and ask for nothing—what blessings they are in our lives. Tamara writes, "I got my German short-haired dog when my youngest daughter was two. He thought she was another puppy and tried to play with her like a puppy does and my daughter screamed in confusion—mommy help! I thought the puppy purchase was a bad idea and hoped the dog would get better with kids. That was in June of 1996. By December of 1996 the dog had grown up and was very happy and loved.

"That December my husband and two daughters—aged two and a half and five and a half—and myself went on our land to snow sled. My youngest daughter told me she was cold and wanted to go to the house. I said let's wait until your sister gets a sled ride. I turned my back to watch my older daughter get a sled ride down the hill and turned back and my younger daughter was gone. We had about a foot of snow on the ground and the walk back to the house was only about fifty feet, but she was nowhere to be found in the winter wilderness. I started to scream her name, 'Courtney! Courtney! Where are you?' Buster my dog heard the tone in my voice and started to run. I thought nothing of it because of my terror of losing my two-and-a-half-year-old in freezing snow. I ran past the house and I could not find her. When I ran past the house on the other side, there was my child getting very mad at my dog for stopping her where she was and licking her face. I ran to my child and hugged her. I gave the dog a hug also for what he did.

"I do believe dogs understand what is going on in people's lives more than we give them credit for. This loving dog saved her life like this about two more times by keeping an eye on her. He also did this for my other child. He is a great dog with kids and we are going to lose him soon because he is suffering from cancer. He will be twelve in April of 2008, but I don't think he will make it. He is one of the smartest dogs I've ever had. He asks us for nothing but love, food, and a place to live, but has given so much. Buster is his name and he will be welcomed in heaven with open arms."

These next two stories of rescue show that animals just *know* when danger is around. The first story tells of a dramatic rescue and of a dog who knew that a little girl was in danger. The second story concerns a little dog giving warning and showing great courage.

Magdalen writes: "I have two stories to contribute. When I was six years old I was trying to learn how to dive in my grandparents' in-ground pool. When I finally got up the gumption to jump, I must have tucked my head in too far and ended up hitting my head on the side of the concrete pool and was knocked out. Even though my grandfather was nearby he hadn't been watching close enough to realize I was unconscious. Well, their huge, sweet, watchful German shepherd Heidi knew what happened and ran full speed, off their two-story deck and dove into the pool (the deep end) to save me. She grabbed me by my bathing suit and swam to the pool stairs. My parents and grandparents witnessed the rescue and ran to my side. I came to and it turned out I was okay, thanks to Heidi. She never left my side the whole summer. . . .

"My second story happened about three years ago. My husband and I owned a large property (twelve acres) in the country in New England. It was surrounded by lots of woods with trails and an apple orchard. At the time I had a twenty-pound two-year-old West Highland white terrier (Westie), also named Buster. He was and is my constant, loyal companion. One beautiful autumn day we were out for a long walk through our property and adjoining apple orchard where the apples were ripe for picking. We came to a little rise in a hill where you couldn't see over the hill to the other side. Buster began to growl so fiercely toward the hill and all his hackles and haunches were raised. I had *never* seen him behave like this before. He was acting ferociously! He started backing up slowly while growling toward the hill. He turned to look at me and then began to run back down the trail we came on; he stopped dead in his tracks when I didn't follow him. He started barking at me with such intensity I knew he was trying to warn me of something. He ran back toward me and started pulling on my pants legs trying to get me moving! Again, this was such bizarre, primal behavior for him! He was such a little dog and he was behaving like a wolf! At that moment I looked back to see if I could figure out what was on the other side of the hill and all I see is two ears and a furry black head—it was a *black bear*! She was eating the apples off the ground. Buster stood his ground and continued growling fiercely trying to defend me. I broke into a run back down the trail with Buster fast on my heels. We were lucky because the bear never gave chase. I have to say we made it safely home because of my Buster. The rest of the day he just looked out the window making sure no bear was on our trail. . . .

"I thank God every day for these wonderful angels He sends us in the form of animals as companions and protectors."

In the stories above we see bravery and courage such as Heidi jumping off a two-story balcony into a swimming pool and then a small dog facing down a bear. Why didn't Buster just think the bear was just a big black blob eating apples? His brain instinctively knew that the bear could bring danger and harm to his owner. This is cognitive knowledge given to us by God and we will all go directly back to God, but I do have some affinity for little Buster since the Westie is one of my favorite breeds and I have one today. They are little dogs with great hearts and courage that will make them stand up to anything, even if it is twenty or thirty times their size. I can just hear Buster saying in trying to get Magdalen to follow him, "Come on dumb owner—let's get the hell out of here!"

Animals Are Receptive

If we can communicate easily with animals when we are on the Other Side, why can't entities who reside on the Other Side communicate also with animals on this plane? This explains how passed over loved ones can send us birds, give us signs, or manipulate pets to do certain things for us while we are on the Earth plane. We must remember that animals are a purer creation than humans; they don't have the everyday problems that clutter our minds. Consequently, animals are much more open to communication from spirits and angels.

Everyone who is successful must have dreamed of something.
—MARICOPA

This next two-part story from a dog owner in Canada relates not only a seemingly miraculous rescue by her dog but also the impact on her son that the same dog had after he had passed away, and how this dog may have been influenced by the Other Side to save her son's life.

Dawn writes, "Our family was at a relative's home on the water, enjoying a fun-filled summer day with other family members. The children were playing in the shallows of the lakeside as the adults watched. Just slightly out of our view, my nephew (age four) slipped away and headed onto the dock while our dog Chum slept silently on the front lawn, totally on the other side of the property. Chum was a very mild-mannered, easygoing, smart Lab who never got underfoot or barked a lot.

"All of a sudden, Chum came barreling through the crowd of family members, barking all the way, ran down the dock, and dove into the water. His unusual behavior alerted us all, and all eyes followed his actions. Within a moment or two he surfaced with my nephew in tow by his shirt collar, dragging him toward shore. Of course, we all ran toward them, finishing the retrieval of the boy from the water.

"I truly believe a miracle happened. Had it not been for Chum we would have all suffered a great loss that day. From that day forward we saw Chum not only as a wonderful companion and protector but as a hero. How did he know about my nephew's distress when he was nowhere near the situation? How did he know exactly what to do when we had never taught him? I guess not knowing those answers may just be the best answer of all! We lost our Chum last year after a memorable seventeen and a half years together. He will never be forgotten and always missed.

"My son is still very, very saddened by Chum's passing, and one evening he cried himself to sleep again only to wake in the morning to tell us that he had asked God to send Chum back to us at night so that he won't cry anymore. After asking me if I thought God could make that happen I simply answered, 'Son, God can make anything happen, but he will only do things that will not sadden or prolong our hurt.' That night was one of the few nights we did not hear our son cry himself to sleep.

"In the morning I mentioned that he must have been very tired and fell asleep fast because he had a better night. He answered, 'No, Mommy, God answered my prayer and let me pet Chum to get to sleep—that's why I didn't cry.' I got goosebumps and was overcome with emotion. He then said, 'Here, smell my hand, Mommy, it still smells like him.' (By the way Chum was a very smelly dog for many years before he died, so bad that he got petted with gloves on at times.) I smelled and I'll be darned if his little hand didn't stink like that ole boy. I almost fainted but dropped to my knees and thanked God for loving my son so very much that he took away his pain with only one simple request. My son still claims to see Chum when he's sad, but not as much anymore. His explanation is that Chum must be needed to help other kids who need him."

As I have explained, I believe animals have amazing psychic abilities, and their sentience and sensory attributes usually far outweigh those of human beings.

In the above story, Dawn wonders how their dog Chum knew not only what was happening but also how to do a water rescue that he had never been trained for. Let's ponder those questions and then try to answer them.

There are several possible explanations. One is that unbeknown to the adults, Chum actually saw the nephew go into the water and go under and then rushed to rescue him. Another explanation may be that Chum's own innate psychic ability somehow kicked in and he became knowledgeable about the nephew's predicament. A third explanation (and the one that I personally feel took place) is that either the guide of the nephew or the nephew's guardian angels made the dog aware of what was going on and directed him to the area to find the nephew, and also directed Chum's subsequent rescue actions by telling him to grab the boy's collar and swim him back toward the shore or dock.

I think in some (not all) stories in this book, the spirit guide or protective angel of the owner communicated with their pet to take certain actions to help the owner or their family. Yes, animals have great psychic abilities, but they are not gods on earth, and in many cases they are nudged by our own spirit guides and angels to do certain things that help and protect us. Also, we must remember that miracles do indeed happen, and miracles are the manifestations of the interference of the Mother God.

Being a psychic, I am fully aware of the paranormal and its manifestations in abilities and phenomena. But I am also a researcher, writer, and teacher. In spite of my spiritual beliefs, I must by necessity have my feet firmly planted in reality. Many people say that one reason why they love my teachings and philosophies so much is because they are not filled with a lot of esoteric ramblings (what I call psychic BS), teachings that confuse and complicate the simple truths that we all are searching for. It seems that more and more "spiritual teachers" are becoming increasingly eso-teric in nature. They evidently think that the more complicated or secretive or elite a teaching is, the greater impact it will have. Nothing could be further from the truth!

The Oxford Dictionary defines "esoteric"

as *intelligible only to those with special knowledge*. Now if you are a spiritual teacher and write a book that is filled with esoteric knowledge and ramblings, just what do you have? You have a book that is boring, limited in scope (remember only those "elitist" few who have "special knowledge" will be able to understand it according to the dictionary), and certainly has hardly any impact. If you, the reader, can't comprehend what has been written, why buy the book? I've always been a believer in giving out knowledge in the simplest manner possible so that all can understand it. I'm taking my cues from our Lord himself, who put forth many of his teachings in parables so that everyone could understand them. I hope my teaching methods are clear and easy to understand.

All dreams spin out from the same web.
—HOPI

The last part of this chapter tells the story of Daisy, who was a heroine with an unexpected twist. Chuck writes, "On a cold winter night many years ago, when I was just four years old, I was asleep with my parents in their bed. Some time later my little sister Brenda was crying from a nightmare and my mom went to check on her.

My mother fell asleep with Brenda while comforting her.

"At some point in the night my mother's dog Daisy began to bark, cry, and whine. I remember my father yelling at Daisy to be quiet. Daisy was a new mother and had a litter of puppies at the time. Daisy would not stop crying and barking, and even though Daisy would not stop, my father fell back to sleep. Daisy then jumped up onto my baby brother's crib and began to bark uncontrollably. My baby brother, who was eighteen months younger than my sister, also began to cry in his crib. The crib was located in my parents' room and my father began to yell for my mother. When my mother did not answer, my father finally got up to see what was the matter.

"When my father turned on the light, the bedroom was filled with smoke. I could not even see across the room. My father ran out of the room to see what was on fire. I followed my father into the living room. I saw flames going up the back wall behind the living room's recliner. My father immediately picked me up and ran back into his bedroom and grabbed my brother who was choking from the smoke at this point.

Daisy was running back and forth barking and crying. My father was yelling at my mother, who was now awake and had my sister. We lived on the second floor and we all ran down the stairs to leave the building. My mother called for Daisy but she refused to come to her. Daisy would not leave her puppies. My mother left the door open and ran down the stairs calling for Daisy to follow.

"I remember standing across the street watching our house burn. I remember my mother screaming for Daisy. The firemen looked for her but were unable to find her.

"The next day my father walked in the door at my grandparents' house, where we had taken refuge after the fire, with the puppies in his arms and Daisy following behind. The firemen reported to my father that after the house burned completely down they were standing by to make sure there was no flare-up. One of the firemen heard crying coming from the burnt debris. Daisy was lying completely over her puppies soaking wet. Daisy and her puppies were not burned at all. Every puppy survived. Neither Daisy nor the puppies had any ill effect from the fire.

244 ALL PETS GO TO HEAVEN

"Daisy was a combined poodle and Shiatsu mix. My mom rescued Daisy from the pound and she was pregnant. After her puppies were born they were all given to good homes and Daisy was spayed. Daisy was a wonderful family dog and lived a long happy life with us.

"I believe that three miracles happened on this day. One, Daisy was trying to wake us up and warn us of the fire. Two, Daisy woke up my baby brother when my father refused to get up from her barking. Three, Daisy was rewarded with a miracle for saving our lives. God bless Daisy for being a wonderful member of the family and for saving my family's and my life."

I'm sure like our angels protect us, the angels protected Daisy. Yes, angels protect animals, too. They don't have spirit guides like we do because they don't have Charts like we do; they are just loving gifts from God to humankind.

8

LOVE AND COMMUNICATION
FROM ANIMALS

"Ask questions from your heart and you
will be answered from the heart."
—Omaha Indian proverb

One of the sad things about humans and
their pets is that human beings tend to
lose sight of the love and devotion that
their pets give them. We tend to take our
pets for granted many times, or we don't
give them the attention they deserve. I know
I am guilty of this at times, when I come
home and I'm tired and thinking about all
that is going on in my life with relationships, family, bills, upcoming lecture tours,
and so on. I sometimes don't notice my
four dogs, who are agitated with loving
expectation at seeing me with their tails
happily wagging endlessly. I do try to greet

them and spend as much time with them as possible, but with my extensive travel it sometimes just doesn't happen. I would imagine that all of us who have pets and a hectic or busy lifestyle are somewhat lax at times in giving our pets the attention and love they deserve.

As we've proven time and time again throughout this book, the bond between humans and the animals we love is profound and strong. But we can learn to communicate with our pets not only through the words we speak and the actions we share. Sometimes, we're able to communicate on a deeper psychic level with the animals in our lives.

Animals Communicate Through Their Actions

This next story really says so much about Tippy and what his owner got from this dog making its way back home. I don't, by the way, believe in chaining dogs, but that's me. I always think, how would I like that! Anyway, it is a wonderful and touching story of perseverance. I think it shows how a pet's devotion and love can override almost anything.

David writes, "I have always had pets in my life and having been raised on a farm I was always surrounded by animals, both domesticated and wild. My pets were 'just pets' and were farm dogs and cats. My dad always loved the dogs we had, but they were always animals that lived outside and were never allowed in the house with the family. Their 'place' was outdoors with the rest of the farm animals. They also had a job to fulfill on the farm as a 'farmhand' to help watch and herd the cattle and hogs.

"I never thought of any of our dogs as an entity with unconditional love toward its master. I believed that as long as that animal/pet had table scraps to eat, water to drink (which was more often than not a mud puddle in the yard or farm pond), and a spot in the barn to sleep, he was happy and could really care less who or what was provided for him. Little did I know that I was about to find out just how connected animals and our pets are to us.

"When I was about ten years old we

had a beautiful tan dog named Tippy. He was a shepherd/collie mix and was pretty large, probably about a hundred pounds or so. He had a long, white-tipped tail and was a very lovable cuddly dog. The problem we had was that he was not a good 'work' dog on the farm. We could not train him to herd cattle or follow commands, unlike the hardworking dogs we had in the past. In fact, he was somewhat of a 'problem child'—Tippy would chase and bite the cattle and pigs and cause all kinds of problems. He would not listen to our commands and would cause trouble with other dogs in the neighborhood. It finally became so bad that, although my dad hated to do it, he said we were going to have to get rid of Tippy. He was causing too many problems and did not respond to anything we tried to teach him. So we put an ad in one of the local farm papers and waited to see if we could give him away to a good farm home that could take care of him.

"Within a week we got a call from a retired farmer whose dog had recently died and he was looking for a nice companion pet on his farm. We made the man fully aware of the problems we had with Tippy, but he was more than willing to work with him and give him a good home. The two of them hit it off right away, and Tippy gave him many licks on the face and kisses. He was always a very affectionate dog and loved attention and gave it back in return. After seeing how well they got along we knew Tippy would be in a good home and decided to let the man have him.

"The man lived on a farm that was about sixty miles away from where we lived and about an hour drive by car. The man had a very large car, one of those big four-door 'boats' that had a *huge* trunk. That trunk was bigger than some entire cars are today! We made a little bed in the trunk for Tippy, with some water, food, and a blanket to lie on. We also sent along his nine-foot chain that we used to keep him tied to his doghouse. I was a little sad to see him go and I think Dad was also. But yet Dad, especially, was relieved that there would be no more cattle being chased, pigs being bitten, and upset neighbors calling when their livestock were being chased at night. We assumed that would be the last we would see of Tippy and we would soon look into getting a new farm dog.

"One week went by and in the evening we received a phone call. It was the man who we had given Tippy to. He sounded very upset and sad. He said he really enjoyed the dog, who was a great companion for him. But that morning the man went outdoors and his heart sank. He saw a broken section of chain and no Tippy to be found. Tippy had broken loose with six feet of the chain still apparently attached to his collar. The farmer had searched the area all morning, but had no luck in finding him. His biggest fear was that his chain may become entangled in a fence or brush and he would not be able to get loose and die. As bad as we felt, there was really nothing more we could do, other than hope he returned soon safely to his new home once again.

"Almost four weeks went by since that phone call and it was an early, cool rainy morning. I had just finished my chores and was in the house waiting for dad to come in for breakfast. Dad came into the house and told mom, my brother, and me to come out to the barn. He had something to show us. I couldn't believe what we saw.

There lying in the barn was the skinniest, soaking wet, mud-covered animal I had ever seen—with a six-foot chain attached to a collar. Yes, it was Tippy. Dad said at first he thought it was a wild coyote or a sick, diseased fox. Then he saw the chain and collar and the tag with his name on it, along with the tan color under all that mud. That poor dog had made a four-week, sixty-mile journey across terrain that he had never seen before. (Remember he had been taken away in the closed trunk of a car.) It was a miracle he hadn't been tangled and caught dragging that chain all the way. It was also a miracle that he even knew how to get back 'home.'

"We nursed Tippy back to health and strength and there was never even any discussion as to what we would do. Dad said that if he loves and misses us so much that he broke loose and managed to find his way back here, that this *is* his home and this is where he will stay. There was no way we could even think about giving him away again. Although he never did become an expert farmwork dog, he was the most loyal, loving pet we had ever had.

**Remember that your children are
not your own, but are lent to
you by the Creator.**

—MOHAWK

"My thought and concept of animals and
pets started to change from that day on
and I have come to realize that they are
much more than a 'domesticated animal.'
They are a true companion sent by God,
with unconditional love to give to anyone
who will accept it. That broken chain and
collar represent to me all the obstacles,
heartaches, and troubles in our lives that
can potentially entangle and snare us and
keep us from making that long, uncertain
journey back to God, our Home, and Family. Only God and Tippy himself know what
was endured on that journey and who
guided him on his charted path, much like
how only God and ourselves know what
we endure on our charted path to the Other
Side. How ironic that, for humans to grow
spiritually and become more Christ-like
and God-like, we just need to open our
hearts and, in a very simple yet key way,

become more like our loving, trusting, forgiving pets."

This next story is interesting on two levels. It shows how the dog empathically took on the same illness as Lindsay, and even more important it shows the absolute devotion to her in her time of need.

Gwen writes, "My daughter, Lindsay, rescued a black dog from the Humane Society more than ten years ago. The dog, who she named Lady, was to have been euthanized the next day. Just last year Lindsay was diagnosed with terminal cancer, and for the past sixteen months, Lady has not left her side. She sits and watches Lindsay constantly. When Lindsay developed a deep vein thrombosis and could not walk, Lady began to limp while she was hospitalized. When Lindsay's leg improved, Lady improved. Currently, she spends all of her time at the side of her bed, leaving only to take 'bathroom' breaks and twice daily feedings. When Lindsay does not wake up for extended hours, Lady sometimes refuses to eat or go outside. Not only does she protect her but she is a comforting companion for her while I am at work during the day. I cannot afford to quit working now to stay home with Lindsay, so Lady stays all day. She is amazing. We have another puppy that plays and plays. Lady will not leave her side. She is so devoted! She is my second set of eyes!"

As we've witnessed time and again, both in this book and in our own lives, animals have marvelous healing abilities, both physical and emotional. We see this with the elderly, the terminally ill, children, and people who are depressed. I've always said that the good part is that animals don't absorb but neutralize negative energy. If I feel bad I'll hold one of my dogs and I can feel the depression or tiredness just seep away. So many dogs, like mine, will not leave you when you're sick, almost as if to say, "I can make you better!"

Melisa writes, "Two years ago this month, I was in the hospital. After my return home, a week later I stepped out on the front porch to see how the weather was and to say hello to Sam, our male Great Pyrenees. Curled up next to him along his belly keeping warm was this tiny, hand-sized Chihuahua puppy four to six weeks old. Sam was being very protective of her and would hardly let me pick up this little stray, but he did finally after I convinced him it was okay. He had to pick her up in his mouth and put her on the porch, because it was too tall for her to crawl up on it alone. So I took her in the house. She was so cold and shivering. I wrapped her in a towel and gave her a little warm milk. She became very attached to me. She has been my saving grace and my therapy. She makes me laugh. She makes me feel better when I'm feeling bad. She even goes with me to my therapy sessions. My doctor gets onto me when I don't bring her with me."

Tammy writes, "I had just turned twelve years old when I got my beautiful wolf sable color, show-bred keeshond. I found an instant connection with her. Precious was the runt of the litter and weighed about four pounds the day my mom and I picked her up. Precious and I formed a most unusual kind of bond; Precious wanted to please me no matter what it took to do so. She had total trust in me, as I did in her.

"Precious grew real protective of me and would lie at my feet at night or in the doorway to my room. In fact, Precious would not let my parents or my brother in my room without me saying it was okay. Precious also knew just what to do when I was crying or just sad. She would nuzzle under my hand with her head, and if that didn't work she would start running at me and start playing, wanting me to chase her, and that would take my mind off of whatever it was that was making me sad.

"I knew early on that she was smart and I had a deep connection with her. I taught her how to count and do math. Yes, it's true that a dog can count and do math! I taught her how to climb straight up ladders to our roof and go over other obstacles. But one day, after we had moved out into the country, she disappeared. I was frantic because she had never done this before. I was very upset until I looked up and saw her trotting across the field with something in her mouth. Precious brought me an orange tabby male kitten home. She heard this kitten crying, I suppose, and must have thought it was in trouble.

"She also protected me in the same loving way. Two years before the incident with the kitten, I took Precious for a walk in our neighborhood. As I was about to cross the street, Precious stopped in her tracks and refused to go any further. Precious kept trying to pull me away from the road, and I was getting really mad at her because she had never disobeyed me! I stepped out to the road, away from the curb, to pet her and to encourage her to cross the street. As I stepped out to the road, a carload of boys barreled around the corner and came within inches of running over my leg. These boys were yelling and throwing things out of the car at me and my dog.

"I don't know if my dog heard the car or just knew something was wrong, but the one thing I knew, she loved me and we had a deep connection with each other. I owed this dog my life, and I made sure she had everything a dog could ever want and plenty of love. She was more than just a dog to me; she was my best friend. I think God sent her to me for reasons I may never know. I loved her with all my heart and never have found one like her again, and I don't expect I ever will."

Tammy's dog Precious was psychic, and Precious protected her dear owner not only in this instance but throughout her life. She could sense that danger was coming, and she probably saved Tammy's life (or at the very least saved her from serious injury). Some dogs if you notice are smarter than others, but I'm convinced that in Tammy's case that it was the time she spent with her dog that made the bond stronger. It's not just feeding and giving water and treats to your pet, but really having them as a part of your life that forges a true bond. You can't make friends with someone you never talk to or play with, or ignore. Why should animals be any different? After Precious died, Tammy was in the throes of tremendous grief and, like all of us, she will never get over her loss completely. But Tammy (and you) can take solace in the fact that we will all see our beloved pets again when our time comes to go to the Other Side. No matter how much pain and grief we suffer after the loss of a pet, we must go on, knowing that they, just like our loved ones who have passed over, will see us again very soon. On the Other Side, there is no time as we know it. While it seems to us that we must wait years to see our loved ones again, to them it will seem only a moment.

Animals Communicate Psychically

This next story again shows how we can have a psychic connection with our animals, but it also shows the kind of bond that can develop between a pet and its owner. If nothing else, I want people to know their pets live on and communicate with them in this world and even from the Other Side—not just nonsensical baby talk but real conversation. You'll be surprised how much telepathy comes to you from the animals you love if you just clear your mind and listen.

Chuck, who we met earlier in the book, had some guidance in realizing his own special psychic gifts as well as how to use those talents to communicate with the animals in his life. "My grandmother reminds me a lot of your grandmother, Ada. My grandmother, though, I believe survived a world much different than your grandmother's. My grandmother and I did not have the encouragement and knowledge of what was actually happening to us with our psychic gifts. My grandmother always called it ESP, and my grandfather forbid the family to speak about such things.

"My grandmother and mother always spoke to me about how wonderful animals were, and how they are living, breathing individuals created by God that have souls. They would point out how animals have eyes and ears and even have babies just like us. They would explain to me how there was not much difference between them and us. They would even tell me how our animals also have ESP. They showed me how our pets knew when the phone was going to ring, or when someone was going to knock on the door. We would observe this time and time again, some dogs more so than others. I had a dog growing up named Dobby who was a Doberman pinscher. She knew every time when the phone would ring or when someone would pull into the driveway. Ten to fifteen minutes before the phone would ring she would lie by the table that had the phone. If someone was going to knock on the door she would go wait at the door. Unlike the other animals that would do this for their specific master, Dobby did it every time. My grandmother would say Dobby had better ESP than she did!

"I did not see another dog like Dobby until I got my daughter's cocker spaniel and started noticing the same behavior. Mandygirl is very smart and understands every direction or command. Since I am a dog breeder I have seven dogs of different breeds. I started studying their behavior toward one another. Once I realized that Dobby was not unique and that Mandygirl also had ESP, I began to test her. I wanted to know if I could communicate with her by body language or telepathy. One day, my English bulldog walked up to me, looked right into my eyes, and said, 'I love you!' I tried to have him do it again but he would not look me in the eyes again that day. A few days went by and Bubba did it again. After the second time I knew I wasn't crazy. This went on for a while until one day my sister told me that every time she comes to my house, Bubba will lay his big old head on her lap and look into her eyes and tell her he loves her. My sister thought she was going crazy because she could hear it, even though no sound was made between the two. I explained that has been happening with me and Bubba for about a year. I told her that I never told anyone for the same reason; people would think I was crazy."

Cherish youth, but trust old age.
—PUEBLO

This proves what I've always said—our animals see, hear, feel, and sense, and have ESP far beyond what we have known. I hope this book helps you watch and talk to your pets more—even mentally. I call my dogs to me mentally if they're out of my sight, and they always seem to respond and come. They don't have to be trained; they just have it naturally, especially if you start at an early age with your puppy. Sure, some are more adept, and it also depends on the amount of time and love you give them.

Alicia writes, "When my brother, Brian, was about two years old, he used a broomstick to unlock the screen door and escape from the house; we couldn't find him anywhere. A little while later we found our Great Dane, Tiny, pulling him home with her mouth around his wrist. My brother was trying to free himself, but Tiny held on."

The above story also brings back a memory from my own life with my youngest son, who was never a problem but who had a tendency to just wander off out of curiosity. One day, sure enough, my son had drifted off. I was frantic and we looked everywhere. All of a sudden, down the street came Lance, our German shepherd, pulling my son toward my house and holding on to his pants with a death grip. After this Lance never let my son go out alone. No matter where he went, there was Lance. Lance wasn't going to take any chances.

The love, devotion, and almost invisible communication that our pets show and pick up for their owners are awe inspiring. In both our stories, the dogs not only had to pick up from their frantic owners that one of the children was missing, but they had to act on that communication or insight and go and find the missing child and bring him back safely, with the child protesting all the way. This not only shows the tremendous ability of animals to pick up and interpret what is going on around them but also shows the deep devotion and love they have for the family.

As I mentioned earlier, stories or incidents involving animals that show great deductive and subjective reasoning can also be the manifestation of communication between those animals and the spirit guides or angels of owners. Even if this is the case, what a marvelous ability to have! Unlike human beings who for the most part do not have a direct reciprocation with God, angels, or their guides, animals are able to receive and have direct communication when necessary because they are a pure creation and their psychic abilities are so advanced.

This next letter proves also what I have said about the ESP that animals have. We could all have it if we visualized and talked to them. It's called the St. Francis of Assisi ability. This saint was reputed to heal animals and, like a Pied Piper, animals reportedly followed him. Heather writes, "I have always had a really strong connection and relationship with animals ever since I was a little girl. Animals are a very important part of my life. I have a deep understanding of their feelings and know that they can understand what I'm saying and what I'm feeling.

"I've always kind of been different—my family members have never really understood my deep connection with animals. I know that I have a gift and that animals are my calling. I can envision my pet in my mind and she will come to me. I think that God sends these animals to me because they know that I will help them. I am currently twenty years old, and all of my life I have always had 'special' and different encounters with animals. I am currently going to school to be a veterinarian. I had known that I wanted to be a veterinarian since as far back as I can remember— hmm—it's funny because my parents remember me telling them that's what I wanted to do when I was five or six years old.

"Right now I have actually been living

on my own with my boyfriend, and since I have moved in so many stray animals have shown up on my front porch. I know that it's not a coincidence and I know that the spirits and God send these animals to me. Stray animals have always come to me even when I was a little girl. I am really hoping to grow and develop my intuitive connection with animals so I can really fulfill my calling."

When my pets get sick I call on angels, my guides, saints, and my passed over loved ones (who do have powers of protection). The thing that most people don't understand is that every person who gets to the Other Side is a saint, not just the ones that churches deem to be.

You already possess everything necessary to become great.
—CROW

Animals Communicate From the Other Side

Heather writes, "A few months ago my mom called the house and was amazed. She had called to talk, like she does every morning. On this particular morning I was out in town doing something, so when I got home I listened to the message and was shocked. Momma was leaving a message and you could hear a faint barking in the background. She stopped talking and said, 'Hello?' and when I didn't answer her she continued leaving the message but the barking continued and got louder.

"After listening to the message I called her at work and asked if she was outside and if there were any dogs present. She kind of laughed and told me that she thought that I answered the phone and our dog was barking. To this day we do not know what or who it was. There is no possible way that our present dog could have interfered with the machine. I personally believe that it was our beloved dog Bobo who passed away some years back."

I often tell people that their passed over loved ones will ring the phone and most times no one is there and the caller is unknown. It's a way of saying "I made it." In this unusual case, her previous pet used an electrical object to convey that he "made it."

Naturally there are some people and animals who have a special affinity for each other, but you will notice that the thread that runs through all these stories is love and love is the binding force in all life. If we have a love connection with humans, why would you not realize it can also be with entities that are far more sentient and, yes, even more psychic than we are? They know when danger is around, see spirits, and love you unconditionally.

In this next story, the parrot was trying to put her claw on her owner's wrist to tell her to stop crying and to communicate to her that *I'm better off than you are and I'll see you again.*

Kim writes, "My blue-fronted Amazon, Peanut, passed away last November. She was eighteen and I knew her since my dad brought her home as a baby; we had to hand feed her, she was so tiny. Years later, after I left home, she moved in with me, and was pretty much a part of my body from the minute I would get home from anywhere.

"I am very sad to say she developed a tumor that no longer enabled her stomach to function properly. She passed away the day after I brought her home from the third doctor. When I found her at the bottom of the cage, I was hysterical and was holding her right away. Even though she was gone I could swear that every time I started to hysterically scream, I could feel a deep scratch on my left wrist. I never saw any scratch or mark, but for three or four times of crying, when I got really loud, I would feel this scratch. This was only within the first hour of crying, because I did end up holding her for four hours. I like to think Peanut was saying—I'm right here—please don't be sad."

Once I went to one of the homes that the famous director Alfred Hitchcock owned because the current occupants were concerned about strange things happening in the house. I walked up to the house, and in a grotto leading to it I got an eerie chill and a sense of two beautiful sheltie spirits near a St. Francis statue. When I got in the house (which by the way had a strange energy to it) I immediately asked the owners what had happened in front of the St. Francis statue. The man and woman looked at each other and said, "Funny you should say that, but two beautiful shelties were found dead at the foot of the statue." I believe these shelties knew instinctively that St. Francis helped and loved animals and made it to the foot of this blessed saint's statue and died. I'm sure St. Francis came for them.

The next story shows how animals as well as people can come back and visit. If they didn't live on, on the Other Side, then they certainly couldn't be seen or come on command and visit. In rare instances people can become earthbound and what we call ghosts, but I've never found an animal that is earthbound. They become spirits on the Other Side and can visit the same way as our passed over loved ones do.

Sue writes, "I work in a nursing home. Last week, one of our elderly patients, a woman who is usually very quiet and spends 90 percent of the daytime sleeping in her lounge chair, began chatting excitedly with an unseen visitor. She had been talking nonstop for about an hour when I asked her who she was talking to. She looked at me and said, 'Oh, that's my friend Mary.' Then she went right back to her animated conversation, completely ignoring me. Finally I said silently in my mind,

'Mary, if you are real please say something about a dog so she'll respond and then I'll have proof.' Within a few seconds, our patient said sharply, 'Oh, get that dog off me! *Down! down!*' and she was gesturing with her hands as if a dog were jumping up to her face. Apparently, the friend had actually brought a dog rather than just spoken about one. I was so delighted and grateful at having witnessed this!

"Later, the patient's son came to visit and I asked him if he knew who Mary was. He said she had been his mom's neighbor, but was no longer living. By the way, the nurse in charge said that the patient had not been given any medication that could cause hallucinations."

The following story about Stonewall not only shows that angels attend animals as well as us, but just as I have told people many times on television that loved ones drop coins, this story illustrates Stonewall knows about the angels, as well as that her father wanted her to find the dime he'd left.

Sharon writes, "Stonewall Peanut Butter Jackson is a rescue dachshund. But he rescued us. He came to us with a bad attitude and a great heart. He quickly learned that I was his favorite, being 'Mama' and in control of not only the food but his favorite thing in the world—the pool. He has surfboards, life jackets, and whatnot.

"One day I was just too busy to go sit by the pool, play with him, and watch him 'surf.' I put his jacket on him and in a sideways manner told him firmly, 'Stonewall, I am too busy, you are just going to have to save yourself and besides, it's March and the water is too cold for Mama.' He looked at me with a grin and launched his little body off the side and I was in a panic. Then I saw something amazing. He dipped his head underwater and grabbed the strap on his life jacket and proceeded to 'pull' himself to safety. I got out there in time to see him looking up in all directions as if he was seeing something I could not. I rushed to him and said, 'Do you see your guardian angels? Did they help the baby save himself?!' He came running over and kissed me so much, I kept saying 'Was it your angels?' He would stop kissing until I said the 'A' word, then he would look and start wiggling and kiss me more. This continued over the years where he would be looking around in a peculiar way and I would ask him if the angels are here; his response is unique and many have witnessed it.

"Today is Wednesday, January 16, 2008. My father passed away on Wednesday, January 16, 1980. It is on this morning that I woke up to an unusual sound. My Stonewall is scratching on my father's marine trunk, which is sequestered in my mother's room down the hall. I went to him and he started looking up at the ceiling again in all directions. I had to ask, 'Stonewall, is Daddy or angels here?' Stonewall let me know in no uncertain terms that yes he was. I moved the trunk slightly and there was a dime. My father had always given me dimes as a child and they have become known as Daddy Dimes. I got my most precious dime this morning from a most precious dog—Stonewall Peanut Butter Jackson, the third."

All these stories give a strong argument for the existence of animals that survive passing and how they do it with dignity and love. Our pets come at a time when we need them the most; others get us through the toughest of times; or others are just our fun and loving companions that are not only part of our life or family but fill a void of loyalty that humans can learn from.

Ileana writes, "Several years ago, I was blessed to have four cats and one dog. One of the cats, Taz, had an extra toe in each paw resembling a small baseball mitt. As a matter of fact, he used to play with one of his many toys, a little ball, and used to throw it against the wall, handball style. The other pets would sit and watch the ball, their heads following the ball, much like following a tennis match, back and forth, back and forth. It was Taz's special talent.

"Shortly after I lost Taz to feline leukemia, I was in the other room and heard the familiar sound of the small ball being 'batted' against the wall and back. I walked into the room, and sure enough, although I could not *see* the ball, I could *hear* it, the sound was there, and the best part— the other pets were sitting in their usual place watching, following, heads going back and forth, back and forth.

"It only went on for a couple of minutes, and it only happened once. But I know that Taz came back that day to play one last game and to let us all know he was still around."

The stories about animals coming back to help people after they have passed are innumerable. This next story is only one of hundreds about how our blessed pets can come back and help us or others, and people wonder why I call them guardian angels (just in a different form) on this planet.

T. writes, "We had a dog named Peanut; he was the smallest of the litter. In 1963 we moved from Santa Ana, California, to San Bernardino, California, and brought him with us. He was a wonderful family member until about 1970 when gas prices started rising and people were storing gas. Someone poisoned our Peanut and he passed that same afternoon. The next day our friend and neighbor told us that Peanut helped him home. He had taken some 'reds' and was too wasted to walk home by himself. My father said it was *impossible* because Peanut had passed away the day before. All these years I've always wondered about things that have happened in my life; thanks to Sylvia now I know Peanut really helped our friend home."

**He who would do great things
should not attempt them all alone.**
—SENECA

Four-Legged Angels

This next story shows that miracles happen also to animals, the same as we get on our prayer line for human beings. Just the other day a woman had called the prayer line in our office and my staff in turn calls others in our study groups and at 9:00 p.m. everyone prays. She called about her cat which had been gone and missing for five years. She called on Monday and on Tuesday, the cat after being gone all that time showed up as if nothing had happened. We get e-mails thanking us for saving their mother, father, child, and so on, so why wouldn't it work for animals?

Linda writes, "I have an Irish setter named Penny. She is now ten years old. She is my best friend and she has a very gentle, loving spirit and personality that make every day on this earth a true blessing.

"This past year she had two cancer surgeries, which included removing her mammary glands from the top to the bottom all at one time. A month later it returned again in the same area and was 7 inches long by 3 inches wide. I wasn't going to put her through another surgery. It just killed me inside. All I had left was prayer.

"I prayed day and night, lit candles, and had many long talks with our God asking Him to please send a Principality angel to cure my Penny. In less than ten days, the cancer was totally gone. Her stomach is flat and the hair has grown back like never before. In my prayers I asked for the angel to pick her up in his golden wings and hold her. I can truly tell you that I have witnessed a miracle that few have ever seen. I thank God every day for my blessings, and know He answered my prayers. Thank you also for adding her to your prayer line."

By calling on the highest phylum of angels Penny was healed. If God looked at animals as just unimportant entities that populated the planet, why bother? It shows God loves and protects all "creatures" great and small. So when you pray say one for the sick or neglected animals; it really helps.

This next story is so touching and beautiful that I had to put it in. I don't think it's important to know where the girl came from or what her family life was about because we have all shared the same feelings of aloneness, abandonment, and loss of self at times. She was just lucky enough to have this beautiful horse that was truly her angel that helped her through many dark days of her childhood.

We don't have to be a child to feel the love and loyalty of animals. I have felt it at the darkest times of my life through loss, divorce, and grief, and yet holding a beloved pet can ease the pain. It's as if they are saying, "I'm here and I will always love and never hurt you. I am constant in my love no matter what the world hurls at you." Yes, as I've said before, they are angels in this life.

Jamie writes, "I was nine years old when I met my first four-legged angel. She was beautiful, incredible, and all mine. Her flaming red hair glowed in the summer sun like perfect marshmallows roasting on coals, especially when she was well groomed or freshly bathed. In her large brown eyes there was a kindness and wisdom known by those who have lived long and well, but with their share of trials and tribulations. Her broad forehead was the perfect resting place for my cheek.

"More than any other place on earth I loved to go to her place. Her place was one of quiet, natural order. Life there had a cadence and a rhythm all its own. It was simple, straightforward, and made sense. The silence there was comforting, not unnerving. It bespoke of peace and calm and was, after all, exactly as it appeared, so unlike the tightly strung silence I was seeking respite from. To this day, the smell of a barn, a tack room, a feed room, dust dancing in strands of sunlight to the sounds of sparrows tending their nests in the rafters fills me with a calming sense of peace I rarely find anywhere else.

"An Aries-born fire-child, I was too proud to show pain or ask for the attention I so desperately craved. With no outlet for all the soft feelings I wanted and needed to give, caring for her in all the many ways a horse needs to be cared for were—although I didn't realize it then—a gift. Cleaning her stall, grooming her, making her bran mash with hot water, carrots, and molasses mixed in on cold winter nights, making sure her blanket was secure, her stall clean, and her tack well tended all allowed me to learn one of the most important lessons anyone can ever learn: to give is to receive. By her example, she allowed me to practice and receive unconditional love, showing me that sometimes the best parts of love are silent, needing no words to be understood, given, or received.

"Horseback riding connected my mind, body, and soul. I didn't just want to ride. I needed to ride. During the years we were together, I learned much about riding and more about life. How I wish I could have understood and appreciated it then as I do now. For it is only with hindsight that I realize just how much she meant to me, how much I learned from her, and how rare and special pure love is.

"When we rode we rarely used a saddle—just a bareback pad or an Indian blanket and we were on our way. The sound of her hooves clip-clopping along as we rode and the gentle rocking motion my body fell into as she moved were medicinal and meditative. On her back I could be anyone, anywhere. I was a rodeo queen proudly carrying my country's flag around the arena at a gallop, waving to the crowd as they cheered us on. I was an Indian princess on my trusted pony riding across windswept plains with my tribe. In the blazing summer sun, I was once an Egyptian goddess riding through the ancient city of Heliopolis on my way to the cool waters of the Nile. Sometimes I was just me.

"She was a natural-born teacher. She taught me about cause and effect. I learned early on that when you ride, if you are not responsible and don't pay attention (cause), you will eventually get hurt, stepped on, or end up on the ground (effect), which generally hurts quite a bit. Over the years, I've discovered that this lesson expands quite nicely to cover many other areas of life besides horseback riding.

"She taught me about patience. She knew her sometimes stubborn charge learned best by experience and never once abandoned me after I hit the ground and needed a few minutes to regain my senses and my breath. Instead, she would stop, turn around, and walk back to where I lay. Standing with her lowered head over my chest, she would patiently wait.

"She taught me about tolerance. Never holding a grudge, with a knowing look, she would wait for the effects of my cause to pass so that we could be on our way.

"She taught me about loyalty during a period in which, even though she was free to roam the acre of land that we lived on, she still chose to lie down and nap below my bedroom window.

"She taught me about trust. How to trust others by how they act, by their body language, and myself by how I felt inside. Sometimes late at night, unable to sleep, I would slip silently out to her stall. She would be lying down near the middle of it and with a soft hello to let her know it was just me she would relax and stay as she was. I would lie down with her and curl up in the nape of her neck, safe and warm. Common sense and training told me that I should never put myself in the direct path of a horse's hooves, especially when they're in a position where they may feel vulnerable. But intuition told me I was safe. Her hooves would not hurt me and she never failed to give me fair warning before she got up.

"She taught me about forgiveness and what it means to love someone because of their flaws and frailties, not in spite of them. She loved me when my moods were dark and my soul on fire. She forgave me when I ran her too long and too hard, fleeing demons that, in truth, were mine alone to flee.

"Together we would run, both of us flattened out and low. She, running full out, her mane and tail snapping in the wind. Me, with my chest pressed against her withers, my legs clinging tightly to her sides, my fingers entangled tightly in her mane, the wind dragging the tears from my face. The power in her muscles was phenomenal—the pounding of her hooves elemental and hypnotic, like the ancient beat of a shaman's drum or the very heart-beat of Mother Earth herself raging against the injustices being inflicted upon her over which she had no control.

"Finally, we would slow to a stop. She carried me through periods of blind terror into places of quiet solitude, places that eased the pain my conscious mind was barely aware of. Both of us winded, we would recover, side by side under a tree, on top of a mountain, beside a stream, wher-ever that particular day's journey found us.

"She was a cooling salve on a festering boil, begat by betrayal, which would take twenty long years to erupt. On those nights I would slip into her stall and lie down with her; she knew instinctively that sometimes a hurting child needs a soft neck to cry into. She seemed to understand the healing embrace of her head resting softly across my back and the soothing heat of the warm air blown softly from her nostrils onto my cool skin.

"And while no one else could see her wings, I could. On some level I knew then, as I know now, that while all God's angels may have wings, not all have just two legs. Some of God's very best angels, in fact, have four."

9

RESPECTING THE ANIMALS
WE LOVE

"It takes a thousand voices to tell
a single story."
—anonymous proverb, tribe unknown

As I have said throughout this book, animals feel joy, grief, anger, playfulness, pain, and a sense of danger, and if that's not intelligence I don't know what the definition is. Because of this, they deserve all the respect and protection we can provide.

Animals are missing the human negative attributes of avarice, vengeance, envy, gluttony, and so on, and certainly don't cause terrible wanton acts of murder and destruction. They do love, they do have courage, they do have loyalty, and they do try to peacefully coexist with others. But sometimes they need our help to survive.

It is no longer good enough to cry peace, we must act peace, live peace, and live in peace.
—SHENANDOAH

In this chapter we'll spend some time looking at the broader animal kingdom and what we can do to protect them—not just the pets we domesticate and keep in our lives but also the wild animals, some of whom need our protection urgently.

Protecting Your Own Pets

One of the hardest subjects for any animal lover to deal with is the treatment of animals. No matter how much animal rescue organizations try to help animals, a majority of the animals they come in contact with are euthanized. While many of us can shout out in protest and anger about this, the fact is that there are just too many pets and not enough owners to adopt them.

Ann Marie writes, "I work at my county's Animal Care and Control facility and while ACC does many, many good things, it is the unfortunate fact that only ACC has the responsibility to deal with the terrible pet overpopulation problem here. This means that people at my facility (not me—never!) have to pick who will go into the adoption program and who won't, and others are responsible for having to euthanize thirty to forty animals per day. ACC gets much negative publicity for this part of its function, and I know that we all hate it, too, but I can't think of a different solution, and I doubt that all the people who criticize it could either, if they bothered to consider the whole picture.

"Most employees have many animals as part of our families, because we try to save as many as we can. Since I started working at ACC, we have brought eight cats and two dogs and eight birds into our family and that is all we can legally have— and probably more than we can afford— but we love and spoil them all and all are rescues. Each one of them is unique, with his or her likes, dislikes, and personality traits, and so interesting.

"Still, I consider my almost three years of working at ACC as time served in Hell on Earth, because I am one of the people who takes the calls from the public, and we have to listen, and prepare calls on animal suffering and animal abuse every hour of every workday. I think the comments I hear most often repeated from people I work with are, 'I like animals much more than I like people' and 'Animals are better than people any day of the week.' And I agree.

"And so, at some point, one night when I had cried all the way home, I wrote to Sylvia and wanted to know *why* so many animals have to suffer, and what they are thinking as they deal with being in our facility. I know it's stressful for them and that they 'break out' with illnesses that they would never get otherwise due to the hardship of being put into a small cage, away from their families (some of whom simply dropped them at ACC on their way out of town or to a new home without a second thought)."

As much as I would like to be able to give all the answers and solutions to the problems that people like Ann Marie face every day, I simply am not God and I don't have all the answers. I can only say that I admire the people who work in facilities like animal control centers for doing what they can and can only empathize with the dilemmas they face on the humane treatment of animals. I don't believe the problems that ACC facilities face will ever be entirely solved, and I know that these brave and pure animal souls do suffer both before and during their "incarceration" (what else could you call it?), and that perhaps euthanasia is the only way to stop the suffering of animals that have been too abused or are not wanted. That doesn't mean, however, that I have to like it.

None of us should like it. The problem is that most of the human population of this world are not that spiritual to the point of recognizing that the Earth plane is only a school for human beings to learn about negativity and to advance their souls by not only surviving it but in trying their best to fight against it. If we as human beings cannot even recognize the injustices and atrocities that we perpetrate upon one another, then what chance do animals have?

The hardest thing about what we call "life" is its negativity. This plane of existence called "life on earth" is only a temporary plane of existence specifically created by God for human souls to experience and learn about negativity. God, being all-loving and merciful, only subjects us to this negative plane for what we might call an "instant" of time when compared to all eternity. The Other Side is our real home and the real reality of existence. The Earth plane is only a school and I'm afraid will probably remain that way until all human souls have learned their lessons so to speak, and have advanced their souls to the point where the school is no longer needed. The cruelty, abuse, and atrocities in the Earth plane are for all to see and react to. Not only fellow human beings become fodder for these acts but so do animals whether they are wild or beloved pets.

The problem has always been one of human desire versus goodness and what is righteous. Although humankind can fluctuate back and forth on what is right and its impact on human wants and desires, we do seem to be making progress. There were no animal and human rights groups to speak of before the twentieth century and now we have a multitude of them. It may take hundreds of years (if our planet and humankind can survive that long), but more and more human souls are becoming more spiritual and loving and the impact of that spirituality and love will have a greater and more longlasting effect on the world. The fact that animals with their pure souls are part of our curriculum just shows us again how much unconditional love and devotion they have for humankind by suffering so that we can eventually learn from that suffering.

For those of you who have pets in your home, think about this for just a moment. Many pet owners are well meaning but not necessarily completely aware of their own pets. Make sure you give them preventative medicine like heartworm medication for dogs once a month and flea protection if needed. Make sure your pet's sleeping area is clean and warm enough, and that there is plenty of water available and only the right amount of food, as many owners tend to overfeed their pets. If your pet is overweight, put him on a diet, as excess weight can lead to health problems or even premature death. In other words, take care of your pet and make sure you also mix in a lot of love and attention. What you put out you will get back a hundredfold—trust me on this.

Sometimes because of our families or our lifestyle, we don't stop and consider our animals and then we tend to take their love and loyalty for granted. Personally I feel we should set aside time to play with our pets and give our dogs and cats love and attention. Sure, we feed them (hopefully), give them water, and maybe a few toys to play with and then just leave them alone to their own way of life. We are not talking about a wild animal here, but one that is domesticated to be part of humankind's life. Now I don't believe in having an animal that is dangerous or destructive. I believe that not always—but most of the time—it's the owner who is just too lazy to correct the dog or cat. I also don't believe in beatings or hurting animals to get them to mind; there are other ways.

We have to respect our blessed creatures and I can't emphasize that enough. This may sound silly, but just imagine if we were cooped up in a cage at an animal shelter waiting to be adopted or just to languish away until we were euthanized or died. I was watching television the other day and I saw a public service message that stated that out of four thousand dogs and cats at this animal shelter, that at least half of them were euthanized because no one adopted them. Many feel that is typical and others think that that number is too small. My dogs have all been spayed. I don't want to reproduce what I can't take care of or save from neglect.

Treat the earth well: it was not given to you by your parents, it was loaned to you by your children. We do not inherit the Earth from our ancestors, we borrow it from our children.
—TRIBE UNKNOWN

Protecting All Animals

From the ancient Egyptians to the Aztecs, Greeks, and even the more primitive tribes of ancient man who painted animals on cave walls that date thousands of years in our past, animals have been revered as well as mistreated throughout our history.

While the reverence for animals as gods by the ancient Egyptians, for example, who also had large grave sites for their mummified remains may be in question, the type of reverence that is given today by those in India or in the Native American population of North and South America is to be commended. Look at how the Native American Plains Indians loved and honored the buffalo. Sure, they killed them for food and clothing and robes for warmth, but they still gave honor to them and only killed them when necessary for survival. This is in sharp contrast to the white man who killed them in the thousands for sport or money in hides and almost made them extinct. Where the buffalo used to run on the prairies for miles, now there are only small herds that are protected by law. Native Americans used every part of the animals they killed to help them survive by making tools, utensils, weapons, food, and clothing. Every part of the animal was used, even the tendons and sinews were utilized as thread and twine to sew or bind.

Nature itself causes some extinctions, like the dinosaur or saber-toothed tiger, to keep its natural balance, but when we introduce humankind into the picture, the animals or species become extinct for capitalistic gain. The hunting of animals for trophies, such as the great mountain apes, is an atrocity. I even saw in Kenya an elephant foot as an ashtray. It's especially shameful now that most of these products can be produced synthetically.

It really makes you sick in your soul when you know rhinos are hunted and slain only because some Asians think their horns contain some kind of aphrodisiac and will pay big money for these horns. Again we see in poor nations like those in Africa, the thoughts about animals and the environment go by the wayside in the face of money that feeds the poor and starving families. Sure, every African nation has put away thousands of acres in their countries for national parks, which is a good thing, but because the countries are poor their budgets for protective park rangers are limited, and poachers do quite a business in almost every nation in today's Africa.

I know that I have talked about our blessed pets, but *all* animals need respect— both those we keep in our homes and those who live in the wild. While spending so much time in Kenya, it was so heart-warming to see how all the animals take care of their young. The cheetahs, the elephants, the lions, the wildebeests, and so on, love their young and try to protect them at all cost. This speaks to a higher intelligence than we give them credit for, and seeing it firsthand is far more exciting than seeing any wildlife program on television. It is one of the many reasons why I have returned to Kenya so often.

All wild animals have their own particular social structures, from the singular animal like the male bull elephant to huge herds of animals like the wildebeest. One of the most fascinating is that of lions. Lions form groups known as prides that consist on average of two to twelve females with one or two males. (If there is more than one male it is called a coalition.) The females usually do most of the hunting for the pride and bear cubs while the males' duties consist of reproduction acts and protection from other males. Female lions will have their cubs away from the pride and then introduce them to the pride at about eight weeks of age. A pride of lions with cubs is a sight to behold as the cubs are constantly playing with the adult lions and crawling all over them. Nature has a way of maintaining its balance, and male lions constantly have to fight off other males who want to take over the females in their pride. It is not unusual for a male only to last two to four years as the head of a pride before being usurped by another male or coalition of males. If this happens the female lions immediately try to protect their young as new male lions will eat or try to eat the cubs of other males. Scientists believe that at least one-third of lion cubs are eaten by males taking over prides. They do this because the female upon losing her cubs is more likely to mate sooner than if she still had cubs. In nature the strong survive and the weak die and this is just another example of how nature culls its own.

The lion and the Maasai tribe coexist; the Maasai take their cattle across the Serengeti Plain and will walk right by a pride of lions and the lions never bother them. If there is a renegade lion the Maasai will go out and kill it, but this is very rare. The cattle of the Maasai are their wealth, which is why they can be fierce warriors since they constantly have to protect their herds of cattle from wild beasts.

I have worked with the Leakeys and other scientists and archaeologists in Africa, and no one can fully explain why wild animals coexist as they do. I feel it's an instinctive contract to let one another exist. Since predators, unlike man, only eat to survive and when they are hungry, their prey can coexist with them. Normally it is the weak and injured who are the ones usually killed.

Jilly writes, "When my daughter was two and a half, we lived in Kariba, Zimbabwe, which is a little town on the mountain with lots of wild animals everywhere. Early one morning, my daughter somehow managed to open our kitchen door and go outside onto the little road, then sat and played in the sand with our dogs. We had to keep our dogs in at night as we had a roaming leopard who liked to steal and eat the pets if they were not locked away.

"I woke up at about five that morning, and knew something was not right. After checking her bedroom and seeing her not there I ran and immediately saw the kitchen door open. There she was sitting and playing with the sand, our two dogs on either side of her, and two meters away (about six feet) there were two young bull elephants, trunks hanging quietly, ears flat against their heads, just standing still and watching her. I called to her to please just walk toward me and, of course, she said, 'No.' My life purpose there and then was to bring my daughter in safely. I thank God and the angels for the strength and courage I received, because, I walked calmly to my daughter, picked her up, and with our dogs following us, walked calmly back into our house. The two elephants then quietly continued their walk on our little road.

"To this day, my daughter has a special bond with animals and especially elephants, and this is probably why she works in the bush in Botswana."

To many of you the above story may seem to border on an amazing miracle, but having visited Africa at least a dozen times because I love it so, I have a special affinity for it. Animals in the wild can be unpredictable, but not for the reasons you may think. Most people think wild animals just want to harm or eat them and under certain conditions that can be very true, but in actuality most wild animals don't want anything to do with humans and will try whenever possible to avoid them.

It is only when predators are hungry or feel that they or their families are in danger are they really dangerous. Wild animals are territorial in nature because of mating and food supply, and those wild animals that are considered dangerous will protect their territory if they perceive they are threatened in any way.

I have witnessed many instances in Africa similar to the above story in which a potentially dangerous wild animal placidly goes about his own business in the presence of humans. I have also witnessed wild animals being dangerously aggressive to humans because they were hungry and perceived humans as prey, or because they felt that they or their young were in danger from humans. One of the first things I look for in the presence of predators is how full their bellies look. If they have recently eaten, they are not nearly as aggressive as they would be if they were hungry. Thus, it is only prudent to maintain a healthy respect for wild animals and to view and interact with them at a safe distance whenever possible.

Do not wrong or hate your neighbor for it is not he that you wrong but yourself.
—PIMA

What Each of Us Can Do

Most of us are too caught up in our problems and own survival to think much about such a large thing as the world's survival. We are concerned about the present and are much more apathetic about the future unless it involves us personally. We tend to be even less concerned about animals, unless we have pets, because we see television programs that depict starving children and the poor in other parts of the world, and we want to fix their problems before any thought of fixing the problems of animals enters our minds. No, the common individual usually doesn't take action, and that is why the influential and the powerful must. Our leaders, celebrities, and governments have to take the lead and then the individual will follow. With the state of the world now, the odds against this happening are tremendous, which is why I think the problem has gone too far.

So what can you as an individual do? Plenty. For starters, we should all remember to have our pets spayed and neutered. There are new statistics that out of every four thousand dogs and cats in animal shelters, maybe two thousand are adopted and the other two thousand are euthanized. This is a staggering number. Now, it goes without saying we should have our dogs or cats spayed or neutered, but people don't because it's too much trouble or costs money or they don't even think about it. It's almost like they think to themselves, *What! My dog have puppies? I don't think so.* (Just like the similar refrain of, *I won't get pregnant*, but we all know how that turns out!)

For those of you who regularly give to charities, try to spread some of your giving to the SPCA (Society for the Prevention of Cruelty to Animals), to nonprofit animal shelters, or animal rescue programs. You might also include donations to wildlife funds and funds to save the earth and its ecology, which are generally all nonprofit and therefore tax deductible. If you are short on money, try to give some of your time in volunteer work to help these types of organizations.

One of the other things that you can do is to become a political activist on a local, national, or worldwide scene. Write and support your local and national politicians who are "green" friendly, and especially support those who take up legislation that affects animals in a positive manner. In the opposite scenario, write and protest against those political leaders who don't support animal rights or the environment. If there are new laws or legislation needed in these areas, write your local congress-man and senators as well as elected state representatives to write bills and get bills passed to change or enact new laws. Ask your friends and anyone who supports this type of legislation to do the same. If at first you don't succeed, continue to try—many times it takes years to get new legislation passed.

Yes, we now have various animal rights

groups that try to protect wild animals, but is it too little and too late? Conservation has always taken a backseat to big business, and despite the efforts of many it still does. Money and power still rule in this world, and huge conglomerates and governments with oil, mining, fishing, and development interests will utilize their vast resources of money and power and continue to rape this world and its wildlife. Humankind may come to its senses and realize the damage being done, but I worry that it has already gone too far, and humankind's predilection for greed is a powerful adversary. Our ozone layer will still deteriorate, global warming will continue to get worse, and more and more animal species will become extinct while a wonderful and precious few people continue to fight for the world and its wildlife against the majority of the world's population, who are apathetic and selfish and careening toward self-destruction.

In many ways you cannot blame the majority of the world for being apathetic, as the vast majority of the world's human population subsists at or near poverty level. You cannot convince a poor worker who is clearing the rain forest in Brazil to quit his or her job because it is damaging the ecological balance and killing countless species of birds, insects, and animals—not when the few coins they earn per day are the difference between their family eating or starving. Survival is a primal emotion that is indigenous in all of us and it will take precedence over ideological thinking in almost every instance.

We cannot blame the poor masses for wanting to survive in any way they can no matter what the cost to animals and the environment, but we can blame government and big business and the upper classes who continue in their quest for money, power, and the things that they buy. They continue to manipulate this world selfishly, and the world and its masses of poor continue to suffer for it. Our only hope for salvation is when the rich realize that they are ultimately destroying everything with their greed for power and money and that they must refocus that power, influence, and money for the betterment of the world and the poor.

**Poverty is a noose
that strangles humility and breeds
disrespect for God and man.**
—SIOUX

In Conclusion

Recently, in our last taping together, Montel Williams and I were talking about the seventeen years we have been together and how the climate of questions has changed. People want to know if they are on track spiritually. Who is the spirit in their home? Did their pet or loved ones make it to the Other Side? We never heard that kind of frank discussion of spirituality or spiritual life seventeen years ago. Now people just come out and say what's on their mind without embarrassment or fear or confusion.

Many say I pioneered this opening up of spirituality, and if that is so, then that was my mission in life for God. So many of the younger psychics call me "Mother Browne" and consider me to be their pathfinder. My only wish is that people just love one another and God and love these four-legged pets and learn from them—to be pure of heart and to ask for nothing but to give all you have in return. You won't be drained in doing this. I believe with all my heart that there is a big contract with God that reads: "If you take care of mine, I will take care of you."

God bless you and your beloved pets because I promise that you will never find the unconditional love anywhere like you will from your beloved pets.

God love you, I do . . .

AFTERWORD

From thousands of stories and letters I've received on the topic of animals and the afterlife—and from the wondrous experiences I've witnessed firsthand—there are many things I know for sure.

I know that we each have an animal totem that protects us, along with our guides and angels and of course God our Lord.

I know that animals see things and feel things that we cannot see or feel. They can detect illness, drugs, and most of all, negativity.

I know that animals can also neutralize negativity in our lives and heal us from anxiety, depression, and pain.

I'm also sure that animals have a real understanding of angels, guides, and even God.

I think the simpler our beliefs are, the easier it is for knowledge to come in. It's man that has given us the fear of death, of damnation, and sin. Animals are just pure lights that God's love can shine through. I'm sure they are here to be an example to humankind and not just to serve us but to show us what we can only find on the Other Side—unconditional love.

Their whole existence is to please us, and each day is forever for them. Their future is always new, uncomplicated, and they live for the present. They even accept pain and dying better than we do. They just seem to know when they need to go, and if we are fortunate enough we see love and understanding in their eyes, and even a sense of knowing where they *are* going and that we will see one another again.

No river can return to its source, yet all rivers must have a beginning.
—TRIBE UNKNOWN

When animals, like your pet, die they don't go through a tunnel like we do. The tunnel is basically nonexistent and many times they can cross a bridge (not always) and they can cross to a meadow and like us they meet their loved ones (other animals). Even though they don't reincarnate (they don't have to), they did exist before on the Other Side, as we did before we came in. Everything and everyone existed before with God, and the reason we came down here was to learn. Our pets also chose to come down with us to act as our guides and to be companions along the way. They are one of our protectors and ask nothing from us except food, water, and, above all, love.

I don't look down on anyone who hasn't had the joy of a pet, but deep in my heart I must confess what I feel is that it is such a loss for them. Sure, dogs and cats need to be potty trained, but so did we, and, trust me, animals are often quicker than humans.

So today or tonight, if you have a pet hold it close to your heart. You will feel its heart quicken and feel the kisses on your face, and with that the promise that animals will never lie or cheat or deceive you. They are what they are—no subterfuge, no mask, just pure love and devotion. As the song goes, bless the beasts and the children.

When you were born, you cried
and the world rejoiced.
Live your life so that when you die,
the world cries and you rejoice.
—Cherokee Indian proverb

NATIVE AMERICAN
TEN COMMANDMENTS

1. Treat the Earth and all that dwell therein with respect.
2. Remain close to the Great Spirit.
3. Show great respect for your fellow beings.
4. Work together for the benefit of all Mankind.
5. Give assistance and kindness wherever needed.
6. Do what you know to be right.
7. Look after the well-being of Mind and Body.
8. Dedicate a share of your efforts to the greater Good.
9. Be truthful and honest at all times.
10. Take full responsibility for your actions.

PASSED DOWN FROM
WHITE BUFFALO CALF WOMAN

Note: She is the sacred supernatural woman who is considered to be a messenger or messiah in Lakota Sioux mythology.

Friend do it this way—that is,
whatever you do in life,
do the very best you can
with both your heart and mind.

And if you do it that way,
the Power of the Universe
will come to your assistance,
if your heart and mind are in Unity.

When one sits in the Hoop of the People,
one must be responsible because
All of Creation is related.
And the hurt of one is the hurt of all.
And the honor of one is the honor of all.
And whatever we do affects everything in
the universe.

If you do it that way—that is,
if you truly join your heart and mind
as One—whatever you ask for,
that's the Way It's Going to Be.

ABOUT THE AUTHOR

Sylvia Browne is the accomplished author of forty-six books, including twenty New York Times best sellers. As a highly acclaimed psychic, Browne consults with police and the FBI to help solve missing persons and other high-profile cases, in addition to her work providing private readings. Browne also founded her own church, the Society of Novus Spiritus, more than twenty years ago. She appeared regularly on the *Montel Williams Show* for seventeen years, is a frequent guest on *Larry King Live,* and hosts her own live show at the Excalibur in Las Vegas. Her son, Chris Dufresne, is also a psychic. Browne and her family live in California.